The Dinosaur in the Living Room

Achieving Positive Change by Tackling the Obvious

By

Harlow B. Cohen

authorHOUSE™

1663 LIBERTY DRIVE, SUITE 200
BLOOMINGTON, INDIANA 47403
(800) 839-8640
WWW.AUTHORHOUSE.COM

This book is a work of non-fiction. Unless otherwise noted, the author and the publisher make no explicit guarantees as to the accuracy of the information contained in this book and in some cases, names of people and places have been altered to protect their privacy.

© 2005 Harlow B. Cohen. All Rights Reserved.

No part of this book may be reproduced, stored in a retrieval system, or transmitted by any means without the written permission of the author.

First published by AuthorHouse 08/03/05

ISBN: 1-4208-2325-6 (sc)
ISBN: 1-4208-2324-8 (dj)

Library of Congress Control Number: 2004195569

Printed in the United States of America
Bloomington, Indiana

This book is printed on acid-free paper.

To my children, Michael, Jeremy and Elyse, whom I love above all else in this life

And

To my wife, Wendy, for her unconditional love and support

And

In memory of my parents, Rose & Nate Cohen

Table of Contents

Preface & Acknowledgements ix

Chapter One   Becoming a Dinosaur Hunter:
Uncovering Obvious Opportunities 1

Chapter Two   Responding to the Demand for Better
Performance 17

Chapter Three   Averting the Sources of a Dinosaur… 43

Chapter Four   Confronting the Dinosaur…. 71

Chapter Five   Expelling the Dinosaur:
Using Punctuated Strategies 103

Chapter Six   Expelling the Dinosaur:
Reversing Decisions & Exiting Negative
Spirals 133

Chapter Seven   Challenging Conventional Wisdom 149

Endnotes: 169

Preface & Acknowledgements

Some years ago, during the course of my consulting activity, it became clear to me that many management teams with whom I worked already knew what to do to achieve dramatic improvements in performance. I found this admission rather odd and even embarrassing (for the managers), since it invited obvious questions such as, "If you already know what to do, why aren't you doing it"? I came to realize just how pervasive and commonplace this dynamic was. It dawned on me that many of the declines in performance were unwittingly self inflicted; and perhaps, were a primary cause of the decline, more so than were external factors or market conditions. I also discovered that despite the awareness and knowledge of what to do, that managers ignored, avoided or delayed taking action. This inaction compounded the problem and added to the organization's woes. Last, I learned that the more effective organizations demonstrated the ability to recover rapidly from their mistakes. They showed signs of resilience because they acknowledged their mistakes, bounced back and learned from the experience.

This book explores and answers the question, "Why do managers ignore, avoid or delay acting on obvious opportunities that would improve performance dramatically; and what can managers do to overcome such tendencies?" The book describes and documents many instances of this paradoxical behavior and draws on more than thirty years of work experience as a manager, executive, senior consultant and professor of Organizational Behavior. The last sixteen years of my career were spent consulting with scores of companies, business units, plants and departments representing twelve different industries and involving more than 200 individual change and improvement projects. Many of my clients were involved in manufacturing and, therefore, a disproportionate number of examples drew from this pool. Almost all of the organizations I worked with had experienced a decline in performance, were losing money or were frustrated by their lack of progress. Because of the nature of these cases and to protect the identity of my clients, most of the examples (with a few exceptions) described in the book are disguised.

My role as a consultant was to work with the management teams to facilitate rapid results, positive change and growth. During the last 16 years, I documented many client engagements and maintained project files that described these organizations, the challenges, the change efforts, the outcomes and my personal observations and insights. It eventually occurred to me that many of these engagements and projects shared some common aspects. To validate my assumptions, I revisited the original files, organized my observations and insights and constructed a possible explanation and framework. The intent was to apply the learning I had gleaned and to share it with management teams so they could avert unnecessary declines in performance; reverse the decline, if it already happened; rapidly generate huge gains in performance; or to simply accelerate the achievement of results. Buoyed by early successes I achieved with several clients, I drafted and published an article entitled, *The Performance Paradox* in 1998. The article became a prelude to *The Dinosaur in the Living Room;* was a first attempt to describe this odd and paradoxical dynamic; and helped to further integrate my thinking. In July of 1999, The Executive Advisory Panel (a group of experienced practitioners) voted and deemed *The Performance Paradox* to be one of the three most valuable articles published in the *Academy of Management*

Executive in 1998. Such positive feedback and recognition showed that the topic was relevant and intriguing to management. Writing a book that built and elaborated on this base of knowledge seemed to be the next logical step.

I think Ogden Nash had it right when he quipped, "Writing is easy. Just pull up a chair to a typewriter and open a vein." There were people, however, that made writing this book easier, and I would like to acknowledge them. First, I have had wonderful clients who opened themselves and their organizations up to in-depth scrutiny, analysis and feedback. Some of these consulting relationships have lasted for more than ten years. And some of these relationships have turned into great friendships. Without the benefit of such relationships and their cooperation and willingness to explore the issues and challenges facing their companies; and without the chance to participate with an organization for an extended time frame, I would not have been able to develop a thorough understanding of the concepts or to glean the insights I did. I regret that I cannot mention by name those clients with whom I am truly indebted, but to do so would run the risk of revealing the names of their companies.

Eric Neilsen has been a friend, colleague and mentor of mine for over twenty-five years. He took the time to review my original draft and subsequent versions of the manuscript and shared his reactions with me. He provided excellent feedback that sharpened the intellectual framework of the book, the concepts and my writing for which I am very appreciative.

Last, I want to thank my wife, Wendy, and my children, Michael, Jeremy and Elyse for providing me with the emotional support and the type of home life that has always kept me going and has served to rekindle my spirit whenever it got low.

Chapter One

Becoming a Dinosaur Hunter: Uncovering Obvious Opportunities

Many management teams know what they should do to significantly improve their organization's performance – not five or ten percent, but twenty-five, fifty, one hundred percent or more. However, no different than persons who know they should see a physician, stop smoking, start exercising or begin dieting, managers avoid, ignore, delay or act contrary to what they already know should be done[1]. I term this odd, but not uncommon dynamic, *the dinosaur in the living room*. Dinosaurs are readily available opportunities that managers knowingly ignore or avoid. This avoidance behavior imposes an artificial ceiling over an organization's potential, inhibits improvement and may be a prime reason for declining performance more so than actual changes in the environment. Like a dinosaur in the living room, such realities are obvious. You cannot miss them. They take up the whole room and are difficult to maneuver around. Managers and employees bump into these burdensome creatures every day. They trip over their tails and cannot get a clear line of sight. People even talk about them; sometimes in public or behind closed doors. Ironically, people ignore the dinosaur in the living room. As such, the organization deals with the same problems repeatedly, engages in ritualistic change efforts or as a last resort rearranges the structure chart. Even though managers know in their heart of hearts that the basic opportunity remains untouched, people pretend the dinosaur does not exist. The following case illustrates this contradictory, but all too common pattern that prevents organizations from achieving huge gains without the advent of new technology, capital or resources.

For five straight years, a supplier of electronic components to appliance and commercial refrigeration customers continued to perform at below average profits. The business was over thirty years old and at one time was the flagship division among twenty other sister companies. Many of the new divisions spawned from this business and were now more lucrative and boasted better profits. To compensate for the loss of product lines that spun off into new ventures, management placed a stronger emphasis on growing the customer base. Unfortunately, as the customer base and sales increased, profits eroded. This trend did not happen over night. It was gradual. Net operating profit declined until the group president, frustrated by the negative trend, sat the management team down and explained that the business would need to achieve a pre-tax profit of ten percent or better. Five percent was no longer acceptable; nor were the excuses. He explained that the general manager and his team had six months to make the changes. Otherwise he planned to make changes to the management team. To cushion the demand, the president offered consulting support to the team and they readily accepted it given the urgency of the charge.

When I arrived on the scene, I learned that the management team was hardly a group of rookies. Instead they boasted an average length of service of twenty years plus. The General Manager had thirty years with the company and knew every facet of the business and every key account. The operations manager had thirty-five years with the company and did almost every manufacturing and engineering job in six other divisions. The sales manager had 20 years of key account experience. The chief engineer had 15 years with the company and was very inventive and creative as evidenced by his Ford Festiva which he Gerri rigged to get 75 miles to the gallon. The controller was the only new addition, but she had significant financial background including many years with a national accounting firm.

To start, I interviewed the entire management team. At the time I was working for a consulting firm that specialized in rapid cycle action projects. This approach aimed to put points on the scoreboard quickly, and to then use the initial success as a platform from which to launch additional and more aggressive projects. For whatever reasons, I decided to depart from the traditional approach and be a bit more patient. After all, I wasn't going to get fired in six months - my clients were. Rather than ask what were some immediate ways to demonstrate progress towards the overall goal of 10% operating profit, I asked each member of the management team, "What positive action might be taken to achieve a quantum leap in performance - not five or ten percent but 50%, 100% or more?" I was shocked by the answers. They said, "That's easy. We have too many of the wrong customers!" As I probed further, I learned that eighty-five percent of the sales were actually generated by the top sixty customers. I learned that the top sixty accounts grew at fifteen percent each year, whereas, the remaining customers were flat or declining. I learned that indirect expense and overhead climbed over the past five years, but were scattered over several departmental financial statements. The number of setups on the plant floor also increased, thus, cutting efficiency. Material cost crept up. Special materials needed for new customers commanded premium prices and minimum order quantities that produced excess inventory. A new plant was added and the existing plants started to look like patchwork quilts. I learned that the situation had existed for five years. All this information was readily available, albeit somewhat fragmented. When asked if any attempts were made to address these issues, they curiously said yes. Such efforts quickly lost steam, however, and succumbed to the belief that sales of any sort were a good thing, since it helped fill capacity. Some of the plant managers and sales people expressed reluctance at cutting the customer base and were quick to share a report that showed that these customers were profitable - at least at the plant level.

Following the interviews and a quick debriefing with the general manager, we scheduled a two-day offsite. The management team was told on the first day they no longer were managers. Instead, they were a group of investors who had just bought the rights to the top 60 customers. They were told not to worry about the remaining customers, since they would remain as an entirely separate business. I explained they had no assets, no employees, and no plants; no anything. Their task over the next two days was to build an organization from scratch around the top 60 customers. They began by developing a set of assumptions, guidelines and ratios from which to work. As we neared completion of the task, I asked them to construct a rough pro forma. The exercise showed that profits would triple, dropping millions of dollars to the bottom line. Silence overcame the room. Some expressed doubt and I encouraged the skepticism. I suggested they redo the exercise and find flaws in the logic. They couldn't find any. I broke the team into two sides to debate the pros and cons and to shoot holes in the assertion. It only served to reinforce and to refine the approach. It became clear that to prune the customer base and to jettison related costs was the right strategy to pursue. Still, people balked at the thought of eliminating customers and millions of dollars in sales. It just seemed counter intuitive and risky. Rather than force the issue and to directly challenge the obvious reticence, it seemed to make more sense to craft some modest strategies to minimize risk and to manage their anxieties. Accordingly, we agreed to carve off several short-burst, punctuated projects. The idea was to test out the assumptions, real time, while demonstrating actual results. In less than three months it was evident that the strategies were on target, and the team could push the throttle forward. Within six months the management team made the changes and, indeed, net operating profit went from 5% to 16%. Return on assets improved from 11% to 19%. The team, energized by the dramatic results, and freed from dabbling with a bunch of low impact accounts, turned their attention to the top 60 accounts. Within another six months they recouped all of the sales lost during the customer consolidation effort. The year was a stellar success.

Evaluating the Importance of the Case

Why is this case noteworthy? There are several reasons. First, it was surprising and unlikely that such dramatic potential could be unleashed in so short a time frame. If someone had told the general manager of that business that he could triple profits, drop several million dollars more to the bottom line, nearly double the return on assets, and accomplish everything in six months, he would have laughed. Moreover, the results were not short lived. Instead, the results met the test of time. The division continued to outperform each prior year for three straight years and continues today on the same path. For example, in the three years following the change, the division achieved compounded growth of seventeen and a half percent in net operating profit and twelve percent in sales each year.

Second, the improvement was achieved with existing resources. Nothing was added to the business recipe. No new technology was added. No Enterprise Resource Planning system was installed. The business was not reengineered. No major changes in management took place. No automation or upgrades to the existing assets were made. No additional capital was infused. No management change programs or fads were launched. Nobody received training. No team building exercises occurred. The management team did not participate in any outdoor courses nor forced to shoot white water rapids. They simply consolidated the customer base, rationalized their plants and jettisoned costs.

Third, the solutions were apparent, known and obvious. A subset of the management team led by the controller knew exactly what the opportunity was and what they should do. Each person on the management team, with few exceptions, could cite specific examples, data, or issues that pointed to actions that would achieve a higher level of returns and profit.

Fourth, despite the awareness and understanding of what to change, the management team acted contrary to the very course of action that if taken, would have improved performance much earlier. This is, perhaps, the most perplexing aspect of the dinosaur in the living room – that everyone or most everyone knew what changes were needed because they tripped over the dinosaur every day. Nonetheless, they acted as if nothing was in the living room. Rather than confront the dinosaur, they avoided and accommodated it. How many times have you heard a manager extol conventional wisdom by saying, "Don't you think if we knew what to do, we'd already have done it? Not anymore, I don't!

Last, I learned that the case was anything but isolated in nature. Instead, I discovered many instances across a variety of organizations characterized by the same dynamic. Whenever four conditions were present, I found that it was a good bet that (like the Labrea tar pits that hid dozens of well preserved species beneath the ooze) an organization sat atop dramatic, untapped potential, yet was knee deep in some form of avoidance, contradiction or denial that prevented the potential from being realized. I concluded that if: a) an organization or business unit experiences a decline in performance after a history of success; b) the management team or a subset of that team knows what to do to improve; c) the opportunity can be realized by using existing resources; and d) the management team acts contrary to a course of action that would improve performance; then there is, indeed, a *dinosaur in the living room*. It should be excavated and confronted. Otherwise performance will remain unchanged or decline further.

Defining the Dinosaur in the Living Room

How do you know if there is a *dinosaur in the living room* of your organization? What do you look for? Are there any indications? To answer these questions we need to explore the four conditions described above in more depth.

Declining Performance

All systems eventually go into decline regardless of their current or past success. Even the real dinosaurs that dominated the earth for 130 million years, far longer than any organization I'm aware of, finally died out. Despite popular theories of asteroids and other cataclysms, evidence suggests that dinosaurs were already dying due to a range of far less dramatic explanations[2]. Organizations are no different. Long before companies go into decline, there are clues that managers ignored the obvious and eschewed the evidence. This is the first hallmark that something is amiss, sometimes known as a blinding flash of the obvious. Such declines, however, are usually gradual and play themselves out over an extended period of months and sometimes years. For example, companies such as General Motors, Kodak, IBM, Xerox, Eastern Airlines and others who, perhaps, were once thought to be invincible, declined, lost market share, or disappeared altogether. An ex-colleague of mine claims he is still waiting to redeem his frequent flyer miles from Eastern. When these companies finally acted, the competitive landscape changed forever and the chance to improve was lost. For those of you who still remember reading, *In Search of Excellence,* by Peters and Waterman in 1982, check out the list of America's best run companies and see how many of those cited, went into decline. A quick review of Fortune's reputation survey reveals changes in the top twenty each year. The comparisons are even more dramatic when reviewed over a five or ten year span. As many as forty percent of the companies drop off the top twenty list - some well below that level. Declines in performance may be due to market conditions, industry consolidation, substitute technologies or other external factors. However, the difficulties connected to the proverbial dinosaur in the living room tend not to be linked to changes in the industry. Instead the decline stems from the way that managers interpret and enact the challenges facing them. This means declining performance is self inflicted despite management's best intentions. For example, a management team may split or dilute its focus; depart prematurely from the original strategy or success formula that made the company effective in the first place; or clutter itself with the wrong customers and products.

In chapter three, a more complete and thorough explanation of a "typology of dinosaurs" that cause a company to go into needless decline will be described.

Knowing What to Do to Improve Performance

A second hallmark of a *dinosaur in the living room* is that the management team or a subset of the team actually knows what it needs to do to improve performance or to reverse the decline. For the most part, I've found that managers have good insights into where the opportunities reside. There are exceptions, but not too many. In the past, I operated under the assumption that the consultant knew and the client did not know. Why else would they need help? Some consultants still operate under that same premise. It's not accurate. Managers, for the most part, are well grounded in their industry and show a keen understanding of their business. They may not always know exactly what to do or how to craft an implementation strategy or to develop an overall game plan. More times than not, however, a subset of the management team can clearly state the changes that are needed to improve performance. When challenged or pressed, they can cite supportive anecdotes and point to data. Elwell Parker was a 102-year-old heavy equipment manufacturer. The company fell on hard times and was eventually acquired. When the new owner arrived, she chose to work with the existing personnel. She explained, "The best resource to confer with is the failing team because they understand the business... and know where it went wrong"[3]. The opening case was no different. The controller and several key managers recognized what the opportunity was. They even discussed it periodically. Remember, the problem is not that managers are lost in space. Rather, they lack confidence in their convictions; are concerned about the risks; are caught in double binds; or have built up defenses to avoid doing what others might ridicule. As a result, they ignore or avoid the very actions that they already know they should take.

Using Existing Resources

The third hallmark of a dinosaur in the living room is that performance can improve by using existing resources – not allocating additional ones. To emphasize this point, I created an icebreaker activity called the *Metaphors Exercise*. I ask managers to describe either an animal, car, vegetable or whatever metaphor comes to mind that captures the essence of their organization's ability to manage and implement change and improvement. I also ask them to identify a metaphor that expresses what they want their future capability to manage change and improvement to become. There is usually a gap between the current and future metaphors. Oftentimes, the gap is significant and amusing. After pointing to the obvious disparity, I ask the assembly of managers to list the changes that might bridge the gap between the current and future states. Typically, managers cite actions and changes that highlight different ways of working (e.g., broader participation or better coordination or less in-fighting or more streamlined work processes or sharing information in a timely manner). Few or none of the responses talk about adding people, allocating resources or infusing capital. To complete the exercise, I ask them, if it were possible to implement many, not even all of the suggested actions; by what percentage would the bottom line improve? They have four choices: a) ten percent or less; b) ten to twenty-five percent; c) twenty-five to fifty percent; or d) fifty percent plus. Without fail, the two categories that receive the majority of votes are categories C and D. A series of surveys conducted with hundreds of managers showed that the vast majority of persons admit that their companies have the potential to produce thirty to sixty percent more with their existing resources[4]. The point, here, is that a *dinosaur in the living room* can be excavated using existing resources. Once accountability is placed where it belongs, it typically is unnecessary to allocate new or additional resources or to infuse capital. Significant gains are possible by simply working differently.

Acting Contrary to a Known Course of Action that Will Improve Performance

The fourth hallmark of the dinosaur in the living room is that despite the awareness or knowledge of what to do to improve performance, the management team inexplicably ignores, denies or acts contrary to the known course of action that would improve the performance. Ample documentation and literature exist that provides insight into why managers act contrary to what they know should be done to achieve dramatic gains.

Many years ago, Jerry Harvey drafted an article called the Abilene Paradox[5]. The Abilene Paradox illustrates a curious tendency of groups to take actions that the members do not truly support. The reason is that they are reticent to voice their actual agreement for fear that others may not share the same belief. The paradox is they do. When Harvey was a young consultant, he worked with a manufacturer that poured millions of dollars into a dead end research project that no one really believed in, but nonetheless supported. Everyone in senior management he chatted with explained that the research project was the primary cause for the decline in profit.

However, the individual members of management never shared their concerns/beliefs with each other for fear of ridicule or worse. Not until the company was at the brink of disaster and the problem became publicized, did the managers admit what they knew all along. Therefore, a sort of *pluralistic ignorance*[6] pervaded the management team. Although every individual was fully aware of the problem, none of them surfaced his/her true feelings and chose not to cross over the boundary that divided private/backstage thoughts from public/group level discussion.

Argyris found similar behavior. He discovered that managers tend to use "single loop" versus "double loop" learning to tackle problems and do not think critically about the actions they take[7]. According to Argyris, single loop learning operates like a thermostat. If the temperature gets too cold, the furnace ignites. If it gets too warm, the air conditioner kicks on. In contrast, double loop learning asks whether the temperature setting was right in the first place. To illustrate the difference, Argyris cites a case of a company that launched a Total Quality Management (TQM) effort to reduce costs. The effort enlisted the help of forty supervisors and produced stellar results. As a follow-up, Argyris interviewed the supervisors and learned that: 1) they already knew which areas offered the best potential to produce results; and 2) they had known of such opportunities for at least three to five years prior to the TQM effort. Argyris contends that although TQM solved the first problem (i.e., cost reduction) using a single loop process, it ignored the second and more fundamental issue; that is, why did such conditions exist for so many years, and what prevented the supervisors from addressing the untapped opportunities. Rather than take responsibility for the situation, the supervisors acted defensively and self-protectively and attributed the inaction to others and to the lack of a program (i.e., TQM). The cause of such behavior, Argyris explains, is due to defensive reasoning and a lack of awareness between what people espouse and what they do in practice.

Citing the work of Hein, Garfinkel, Shaw and Blum, Weick[8] provides an understanding of how managers create artificial barriers and limitations that prevent them from acting on apparent opportunities. In large part, limitations exist because "managers fail to act, rather than fail while they are acting"[9]. They unwittingly collude to avoid testing to see if change is, indeed, possible. Instead, they justify this avoidance behavior by erecting rationales for why no action was taken or for why an opportunity remains untested. Thus, it is on the basis of avoidance, speculation and untested assumptions that managers conclude that obstacles and roadblocks exist. Such imagined or artificial constraints become self-imposed injunctions that managers factor in, when faced with problems such as declining performance. Over time as managers see each other avoid the same issues and activities, they assume that the inaction is based on real impediments. Such observations are deemed to be lessons learned. In reality, the conclusions surrounding the avoidance never were tested or experienced, first hand. For example, a manufacturer of injection molding machines repeatedly accepted orders for unprofitable machines under the assumption that burden was being absorbed. In reality, they lost money. However, when faced with the same decision week after week and month after month, no one ever killed such orders and, therefore, never discovered what the real impact might be. For reasons like these, Weick concludes that "…problems that never get solved, never get solved because managers keep tinkering with everything, but what they do"[10].

In a more recent study conducted by Ffeiffer and Sutton, the authors found that a significant gap between knowing and doing exists. Their assertion is that the so-called knowledge advantage is a fallacy[11]. Whereas tremendous effort and resources focus on the acquisition of knowledge, too little effort centers on the implementation or use of that knowledge. Citing both original research and the work of others, they learned that very little change or results occurred in many instances despite huge investments in training, business literature, knowledge management, storage and retrieval systems or the awareness of well publicized best practices. For example, they asked managers of a large restaurant chain to list and rate best practices that were key to successful financial performance. They asked the same managers to rate the extent to which such practices were actually followed and implemented. In seventeen out of twenty-five practices, they discovered statistically significant differences between what the managers knew should be done and what they actually implemented. The results of their study were repeated across other industries with similar findings. To quote Ffeiffer and Sutton, "Time after time people understand the issues, understand what needs to happen to affect performance, but don't do what they know they should"[12].

Summary

John Kotter explained, "The change problem inside organizations would become less worrisome, if the business environment would soon stabilize or at least slow down. But most credible evidence suggests the opposite…"[13] Since the business environment is unlikely to stand still anytime in the near future, it makes sense to start by targeting obvious opportunities that hold huge potential to improve performance. If managers confront the avoidance behaviors (just like you would in therapy), they could paradoxically *avoid* complex, ineffective, protracted and labor-intensive change efforts. They could reduce their dependence on outside change programs and expertise. They could limit their participation in contrived rituals; and they could target higher payoff opportunities that would improve performance dramatically or reverse the inevitable declines in performance that all organizations eventually experience. This is easier said than done, however, since such behavior is all too human. It is, nonetheless, possible, with concerted effort, to overcome such tendencies and to produce extraordinary results in comparatively short time frames. Save the fancy change efforts and sophisticated tools for the tough stuff. In the meantime, put points on the scoreboard now and give your team a fighting chance to win.

Chapter Two

Responding to the Demand for Better Performance

At the same time that management teams struggle to achieve positive change and results, they often ignore immediate opportunities that, if taken, would improve performance significantly. So what? Isn't that just human nature to act in contradictory ways and there is nothing we can do about it? Yes, it is human nature and no, we cannot *ignore, avoid or make excuses* because some very noteworthy changes took place that make it essential to capture every opportunity to improve performance that we can. To fully understand why *confronting the dinosaur* and tackling obvious opportunities should become a key part of any improvement arsenal, it is useful to grasp how the managerial landscape changed and why such changes warrant different, higher payoff and less labor-intensive interventions for producing results and positive change.

Less Time to Do More Work with Fewer People

Over the last decade and a half, one trend seems clear. *There is less time in which to accomplish more work with fewer people.* Almost everyone with whom I work complains about not having enough time to complete his/her tasks amid growing demands, let alone launch another change effort. In the past, I heard similar complaints, but often dismissed the words as excuses and, therefore, pushed ahead with the client to carve off improvement projects to achieve the desired results. This time it's different. The complaint is valid. The time available in which to conduct change and improvement projects is limited even before you get started. A survey by the American Management Association conducted in mid 1995 found that more than one half the respondents felt overwhelmed by work... A similar survey done in Britain discovered that 70% of workers felt less secure; 44% felt pressure to work late; and, 31% said they were afraid to take time off even when sick[1]. In the new millennium, I suspect such findings are even more severe.

There are four main forces (i.e., the pressure to grow; the demand for cost reduction; industry consolidation; and the emphasis on speed and cycle time) that are driving this dramatic shift, shaping a change in sentiment and promoting a set of conventional responses that are off base.

Four Forces Driving the Demand for Better Performance

The Pressure to Grow

There is clearly an imperative for companies to grow, be operationally effective and to remain competitive. No one is sufficiently secure as to be immune from the need to grow and improve. As one executive explained, "If you are not growing, then it means you are declining". Christian and Raynor explain one reason why there is such an enormous pressure to grow. "Despite a company's success, its executives soon realize that they face a growth gap. This is caused by the pesky tendency of Wall Street investors to incorporate expected growth into the present value of a stock – so that meeting growth expectations results only in a market-average rate of stock price appreciation. The only way that managers can cause their companies' share price to increase at a faster rate than the market average is to exceed the growth rate that investors have already built into the current price level. Hence, managers who seek to create shareholder value always face a growth gap – the difference between how fast they are expected to grow and how much faster they need to grow to achieve above average returns for shareholders"[2].

In addition, more and more companies are owned by venture capitalists and private equity (PE) firms than in years past. I have consulted to companies owned by such firms and the game is, indeed, different. For example, such organizations have more aggressive growth and profit expectations than other companies do, because the private capital they've raised is based on expectations of high risk and high return. And the individual investors in such funds are not your ordinary investors. They expect more in less time. In addition, the time frame for results is typically only three to five years because the PE firms or venture capitalists plan to sell the acquired companies and want to ensure a healthy return.

Last, many North American industries are mature and have seen or are seeing their growth rates slow and flatten. For example, the *Corporate Strategy Board* shared a study that shows that of the 172 companies that were listed at one time on Fortune's 50 largest companies between 1955 and 1995, ninety-five percent saw their growth rates drop at or below the rate of GNP growth. Of those companies that experienced this stagnation, only 4 percent were able to boost their rate of growth to just one percent above GNP growth. When growth slows, executives and investors get anxious and impatient and place increased pressure on the management team to do something.

The Demand for Cost Reduction

Confronted by growing competition, a global economy, over capacity, slower growth rates and aggressive investors, many companies turn to downsizing, restructuring and reengineering to remain cost effective. For example, in 1993, large U.S. firms cut nearly 600,000 jobs. This figure was 25% higher than it was in 1992. And 1992 represented a 10% increase over 1991[3]. Companies such as Seagrams, Owens-Illinois, Monsanto, Union Carbide, IBM, Kodak and others reduced headcount by 10% or more while dozens of other organizations decreased headcount between 5% and 10% (e.g., BASF, Westinghouse, Borden, General Motors, etc.)[4]. In 1994 another 516,000 jobs were eliminated and $10 billion was spent to restructure. Firms like Mobil, Proctor and Gamble, GTE, Glaxo-Wellcome and Sara Lee joined the downsizing and reengineering craze to remain competitive[5]. In 2003, the payroll report estimated that some 2.4 million jobs were lost. Each year the same firms cut a bit more, outsource additional operations or consolidate jobs, functions and business units. A study performed by the American Management Association found that two-thirds of those companies that downsized did so again the following year; and 25% of those surveyed reduced staff in three or more of the next five years. Be mindful that such job eliminations took place during one of the longest and most prosperous economic cycles from 1991 to 2000. The same trends continue, as more jobs are lost to lower cost labor markets such as China and India. And many of these jobs are not coming back because of the gains achieved in productivity and new technology.

The Pace of Industry Consolidation

The pace and number of acquisitions, mergers and industry consolidations that occurred throughout the '90's was dramatic. General Electric alone reported in its annual report to shareholders that the company acquired over 110 companies in 1999. According to investment bankers, J.P. Morgan, companies worldwide spent $3.3 trillion on mergers and acquisitions in 1999[6]. This figure represents an increase in spending for acquisitions of 32% over 1998. In 1995 the high-tech industry alone consummated 2913 mergers compared to 1861 mergers and acquisitions done in the prior year.

Someone must integrate these acquisitions once due diligence has been conducted and the deal is signed. The task of integrating new businesses is often underestimated. It is a full time, all consuming activity that is frequently added to the already full plates of many departmental and business unit managers. As managers focus their efforts on offsetting the premium paid in excess of the market value for the acquired company, they time and again implement further cuts in headcount to achieve the desired returns. In addition, as industry consolidation takes hold due to deregulation and over capacity, suppliers find that the customer base shrinks due to no fault of their own, thus, making it even more difficult to achieve arbitrary growth targets imposed by investors and senior management.

The Emphasis on Speed and Cycle Time

At the same time that workloads increased due to reductions in headcount, industry consolidation and the acquisition frenzy, the demand for speed became paramount. Fueled by the quality movement of the 1980's, and further refined in the 90's by approaches such as lean thinking, value stream mapping and reengineering, speed and cycle time dominated managerial thought. As products matured, quality improved and the installed base of product in the field increased by multiples many times the level of new product sales, the focus shifted to speed, service and convenience. Product life cycles decreased. Just look at the disk drive industry. From 1975 to 1992, disk drives were replaced by smaller versions that moved from fourteen-inch to one point eight inch disk drives. And the pace at which the capacity and density of each disk drive improved was greater than its predecessor after its introduction[7]. Order-to-ship cycles decreased. Lead-time for new product development fell. For example, not long ago the platforms for automobiles lasted 10 years. Today, the life of a platform lasts only two to four years before it is dated. Toyota boasts that you can order a car and have it completed and shipped within several days. Set up time that took months now occurs in minutes. And with the advent of the Internet, information became instantaneous. Examples other than manufacturing also exist. Consider Taco Bell, the fast food chain. Using reengineering techniques, Taco Bell redesigned its food delivery process and improved service during lunchtime hours by seventy-one percent or just thirty seconds[8]. The New York Transit Police organization dramatically reduced more than 8000 administrative forms to a fraction and used video conferencing to save time testifying in court[9].

Responding to the Demand for Better Performance: Four Misguided Responses

Exhibit 1 shows that the convergence of the four forces described above (i.e., the pressure to grow; cost and headcount reduction; industry consolidation characterized by frenzied acquisitions; and the emphasis placed on speed and cycle time) prompted managers and executives, desperate for help and support, (because they had less time to do more work with fewer resources) to search for remedies and answers that were quick and required little direct involvement or critical thinking. Unfortunately, managers resorted to four misguided responses while trying to meet the demand for better performance. These included: succumbing to growth traps and managerial pitfalls; over-relying on external change programs; implementing total systems change efforts; and minimizing risk & acting defensively.

Succumbing to Growth Traps & Managerial Pitfalls

Although well intentioned, many efforts and attempts to grow turn into self inflicted wounds that cause organizations to go into decline unnecessarily. Such decisions precipitate a decline in performance because they unwittingly push the organizations off course strategically; or they introduce competing priorities that pull their organization in conflicting directions. In essence, the responses are fundamentally flawed. Examples of growth traps include decisions to prematurely abandon an organization's success formula or business model; or that clutter and complicate an organization with unprofitable customers and products; or that improperly leverage a company's core competency into unfamiliar

Exhibit 1:

Responding to the Demand for Better Performance: Four Misguided Responses

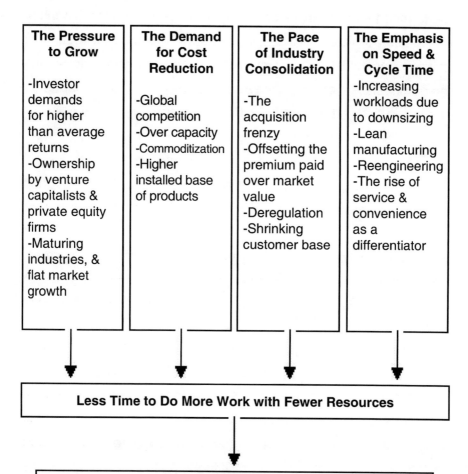

markets & customers just to fill capacity without regard to strategic fit; or that allow self interest and ego to eclipse organizational welfare. These examples are described in greater detail in chapter three. Once such decisions are made, however, the management team is often reluctant to acknowledge the mistake and to reverse course. This avoidance and self protective behavior is exactly what gives rise to a dinosaur in the living room.

Over Relying on External Change Programs

Contrary to many who believe otherwise, and despite extensive advertising, the track record for change programs is abysmal. Over the past decade, I've made a hobby of collecting studies, books and articles that assess the effectiveness of change efforts and management fads. The findings are chilling. Based on studies conducted by such notables as McKinsey, E&Y, A.D. Little and Rath and Strong, it appears that the success rate for change efforts and programs in the last decade ranges somewhere between one in five to one in three. This means the failure rate is a staggering 70 to 80 percent. For example, one survey conducted by the American Electronics Association of 300 electronic companies showed that less than one third of the 85% of the companies that had implemented quality programs achieved any positive results. In another study performed by McKinsey & Company, they found that two-thirds of quality programs failed to yield any real improvements[10]. Even in the automotive industry where the quality revolution spawned, many suppliers still do not use flexible manufacturing systems or measure up to the quality standards set. Just look at the Firestone tire debacle. In an article published in Harvard Business Review, the findings revealed that in a study of one hundred companies that launched reengineering efforts, little if any gains in overall business results appeared. Twenty of the firms researched showed that the majority achieved less than a five percent improvement and only six of the one hundred companies achieved reductions of 18% in overall costs. A survey conducted by A.D. Little found that only 16% of managers who engaged in reengineering were fully satisfied[11]. Even James Champy and Mike Hammer, the architects of reengineering, acknowledged that the efforts were not producing the desired results. Based on a study done involving 4000 focus groups, Sibson and Company discovered that both employees and customers rated the effectiveness of management fads their companies had used between 10% and 20%. In a 1994 HBR article[12], Nohria and Berkley observed that U.S. market share, calculated as a percentage of worldwide sales, steadily declined over the last three decades for the twelve largest companies in each of seven different industries, concurrent with a dramatic rise in the management industry (i.e., consulting, business schools, journals, training, etc.). Whereas the fads are certainly not the cause of the decline, the so-called solutions and panaceas failed to abate the free-fall or to solve the company's loss in market share despite growing world markets. It does not appear that the reliance on such change and improvement efforts will abate any time soon.

So why did managers turn toward such programs when the record was questionable? Beer, Eisenstat and Spector offer an answer to the question, "Why has there been an over reliance on such approaches and why are these so appealing to managers[13]. To start, the change programs can be put into place quickly because they are already designed and ready to go. Second, managers like to emulate success stories, even if the context or circumstances are different. Third, the change programs and packages appear easy to measure. Unfortunately, the measures usually track activities and not meaningful results. Last, the programs can be delegated to staff or consultants while line managers go about the task of day-to-day activities.

It is, therefore, no surprise that during the past twenty years we've seen a rise in the management industry. Consulting firms, training, management schools, MBA programs and business media grew at double and triple digit rates, some as much as 400 percent[14]. Anderson Consulting alone generated over 3.5 billion dollars a year. There are over 100,000 consultants employed in the field and business schools number in excess of 700. Despite the availability of an entire field dedicated to helping a company achieve better performance, the results have yet to justify the expenditures.

Implementing Comprehensive Change Efforts or Total Systems Solutions

Rather than work with existing resources, many management teams assumed that something more radical or comprehensive was in order. As such, managers turned their attention toward large scale, complex or total systems change efforts. Believing that an organization wide solution will finally put all the puzzle pieces together and provide the results they all sought, many managers forgot that there was less time to do more work with fewer resources. Undaunted by the limitations, they plowed ahead thinking the new system would improve performance. Instead, they confronted the stark realization that tackling such an ambitious undertaking quickly overwhelmed the organization; exceeded the capacity of the company to absorb the volume of changes; discovered that there was no one to do the work; and learned that the new system could not deliver the expected returns because the underlying processes were never changed.

For example, a manufacturer of hand held data entry devices and bar coding technology decided to install an enterprise resource planning system (ERP) to boost performance. After two years, the installation was behind schedule and several million dollars over budget. The project leader, a senior executive of the firm, asked us to determine and benchmark what return should be expected. The results of our benchmarking activity revealed that no return on investment (ROI) data was available. We discovered that the only information contained in a two and one half inch thick binder and research study of ERP systems, at the time, was largely anecdotal and cited sporadic results on a case by case basis. No systematic assertions to support that a return on investment was possible were found! The executive who commissioned the benchmarking study never asked us to work with her to accelerate the project deliverables or to focus the effort on achieving results. She was so invested (literally and figuratively) in the systems and software that she forgot about actual performance. Two months after our departure she was, not surprisingly, fired.

Acting Defensively and Self Protectively...

Several years ago I worked with a fiberglass manufacturer who hired us to design a change effort to improve furnace efficiency. Of the two furnaces housed within the plant, one furnace performed far below industry standard. P*ounds packed* were a critical measure of success, especially in this commodity driven business. Every percentage point of efficiency added $18,000 of operating profit per month. Furnace efficiency limped along at 68%. As management explained, "When the economy turns favorable, we have to achieve higher productivity; otherwise we incur expensive tolling charges by outsourcing to competitors to meet customer demand". The under-performing furnace ran a specialty type of glass that normally warranted more staff and stringent safety requirements. In chatting with the staff from the forming room, research lab, maintenance and process engineering, it became clear that everyone felt that if more staff were added, efficiency would improve. The plant manager appeared to be the only hold out and resisted any effort to increase staff. Still, the advocates all explained that the gains in efficiency would more than offset the cost of adding forming room employees. To quote one process engineer, "I am willing to bet my job that we'll add ten points of efficiency, if we just add the right complement of people. If it doesn't work, they can fire me!" Everyone tried to convince the plant manager to add staff, but he simply dug in his heals.

Why was the plant manager in denial? Was he genetically predisposed to such behavior? No! It was nothing of the sort. After probing and poking, it came to light that corporate mandated a cut back earlier in the year. The plant manager was forced to reduce direct labor. This action was hotly contested. Although he did not support the action, he complied and acted like a good corporate citizen. When confronted with the dinosaur in the living room (i.e., adding back the staff he cut), he felt he would lose face with the union and employees and, therefore, resisted reversing the earlier decision. After weeks of coaxing and discussion, he finally agreed to add staff, but only as a test. He insisted that the recall of employees be classified as temporary, rather than full time permanent. Once staffing in the forming room returned to the desired manning levels, efficiency climbed twelve percentage points and net-operating profits jumped over $2.5 million per year.

This case shows that managers who act defensively are not blind or unaware. They are often well aware of the situation as the plant manager was. They know what actions might work. They simply adhere to a different logic that is designed to minimize risk. The plant manager, described above, felt trapped and acted cautiously. Months earlier he cut staffing levels. Now, he had to reverse the decision and risk losing face or looking stupid. So he chose to live with sub-standard results by avoiding a decision. Top management who mandated the cuts was nowhere to be found. He was the one left holding the bag and he had no intention of compounding the original sin. Before he was willing to even consider reversing his earlier decision, he needed the safety of knowing that the recall of employees would be temporary, rather than permanent, so if needed, he could maintain flexibility.

After being beaten up for not achieving growth expectations; after surviving cost cutting and headcount reductions; after being overwhelmed by total systems change efforts that force people to work 65 and 70 hours a week with results that do not even begin to approximate the investment of time and money; and after relying on outside change programs that sound good, but leave much to be desired; is it any wonder that managers act defensively?

Re-Aligning the Responses…

Given the track record and potential for misguided responses, one might conclude that management teams will rarely be able to confront a dinosaur or capitalize on obvious opportunities or achieve dramatic results. However, this conclusion does not account for the dramatic success stories that exist. Some management teams did, indeed, learn how to reverse declining performance, take advantage of immediate opportunities, confront flawed decisions or exit negative spirals in which they were caught. In retrospect, these successes reveal four important insights. First, the management teams discovered that declines in performance were due to specific actions that they took or did not take – not to any environmental or external forces. Second, they fully embraced the idea that just because people knew what to do to improve performance or to reconcile a flawed decision, there was no guarantee that action would occur. Something more was needed. Third, they recognized that a primary reason for inaction and avoidance was due to self protective or apprehensive behavior; often prompted by the anxiety connected to the intense demand for better performance, less available time, greater workloads or fewer resources. Last, the management teams realized that reducing anxiety to a tolerable level was a precursor to mobilizing action and expelling a dinosaur.

How can we apply such insights to design change methods that acknowledge these important behavioral realities, while also building more resilient organizations (defined as the ability to recover rapidly from mistakes)? There are three guidelines and change practices to follow, if we are to achieve better performance and to avoid the pitfalls of a misguided response:

1. Avert the Sources of a Dinosaur and the Causes of Needless Declines in Performance

To start, it would be nice, if we could avert needless declines in performance altogether and eliminate the sources of a dinosaur in the living room. Doing so would divert vast amounts of wasted time and effort toward positive change and results. To achieve this outcome, however, we first have to have an in-depth understanding and awareness of what the causes and sources of a dinosaur are. For example, Darwin Smith and his management team from Kimberly-Clark decided to sell its paper mills and to do battle in the consumer products market because they realized that the traditional core business - coated paper - was doomed to mediocrity. All of his predecessors ignored this fact, pursued safer growth strategies and, therefore, remained stuck at a mediocre level of performance. Charles Walgreen faced a similar and, perhaps, tougher challenge. He made the decision to exit the food service business (a family legacy) and to focus solely on convenient drugstores, rather than allow the two business concepts to compete for limited resources. The cumulative stock returns for Kimberly-Clark and Walgreen improved to 4:1 and 16:1, respectfully; far in excess of how other companies performed over the same time frame. Although both executives could have succumbed to a variety of growth traps or followed the same well-worn path of lack luster performance, they averted them by sharpening the focus and making bold, albeit clear, decisions. When a management team learns to avoid such traps and instead focuses its time and energy on high payoff opportunities, it unleashes huge potential.

2. *Confront the Dinosaur: Making It Possible to Discuss Difficult Issues Openly...*

It is not always feasible to avert a dinosaur or needless declines in performance. As such, we have to make it possible and safe to openly talk about difficult issues that have been ignored, avoided or denied. Developing the capacity to talk openly and freely about tough issues will allow management to confront and reconcile mistakes rapidly and to minimize harmful avoidance behaviors. Remember, managers pretend that a dinosaur is not in their living room, not because they cannot see it, but because they do not want to see it. Consider the following example:

A combination metal former and powder coater experienced high scrap and quality defects. Management launched a series of short-term projects to address the problems. Within a few months they produced some modest gains. The initial success obscured the underlying issue connected to scrap and defects, however. Closer review showed that the business added a new powder coating line to increase its capacity to allegedly grow and add customers. Once the asset was up and running, management moved rapidly to fill the additional capacity with new customers and different products so as not to lose money. Unfortunately, the new products were limited to powder coating only – not metal forming. The management team shifted the focus from products in which they had expertise to ones where they had less capability and competence. The existing base of profitable products competed on the basis of metal forming and powder coating; not just a single operation. This made it more difficult to price products competitively, since the new products only required powder coating. In addition, introducing products that only needed powder coating added new complexity to scheduling, routing and logistics, thus, shortening production runs and increasing scrap due to start-up. In less than six months after they launched the scrap reduction projects, they found that scrap had again escalated to unacceptable levels. The results were short lived.

After a series of interviews revealed that many members of the management team felt that acquiring a new powder coating line was a mistake, they owned up to the fact that they had compounded the problem by adding products that extended beyond their competency just to fill capacity. Once the unspeakable dinosaur was given voice, they were able to shift their focus to searching for a way out of the mess. Since they were no longer constrained by an assumed gag order, they implemented a very different set of projects that virtually eliminated scrap, strengthened the strategic direction and returned the firm to higher earnings. As the example shows, the management team finally accepted accountability for the source of the dinosaur in their living room and expelled it. Until they did so, little or no progress was possible.

3. Expel the Dinosaur: Two Methods for Reducing Anxiety to Tolerable Levels & Mobilizing Action...

Even when managers or executives acknowledge the presence of the dinosaur, it is still hard to mobilize action. Although a management team may show awareness, accept accountability or admit that they've ignored or avoided an obvious opportunity, there is no guarantee they will act. Many managers tend to be wary, risk averse or self protective, sometimes for very good reasons. We, therefore, have to find ways that enable people to make new choices to expel a dinosaur from their midst. Promoting this type of action requires that we reduce anxiety to tolerable levels. Two change practices, in particular, have proven to be very effective: 1) Using punctuated strategies to achieve incremental gains; and 2) Reversing flawed decisions and exiting negative spirals.

Using Punctuated Strategies to Achieve Incremental Gains...

People are more willing to take action and risks, if the scope of a change effort is limited, manageable and phased. This approach offers perceived protection and, thus, lowers anxiety, while still making incremental progress possible. For example:

A stock transfer group of a major banking organization wanted to grow. At the time, the division was the fifth largest stock transfer businesses in the United States representing high profile, publicly traded companies. Unfortunately, the business experienced a growing backlog of aged correspondence to shareholders. In addition, the outgoing correspondence to shareholders contained many errors and mistakes. Not only did this situation produce complaints from many top executives that were clients, but the Securities Exchange Commission expressed concern and urged the company to solve the problem; otherwise, they would have to intervene. These issues were not new and had existed for well over a year. The threat of SEC intervention prompted management to finally act. We were brought in to work with the staff to reduce the errors, decrease the backlog of aged correspondence and to allay the concerns of the SEC, shareholders and the client companies. To start, we worked with management to target one department where progress would produce an immediate and positive impact. With our help, they carved off a short term, razor sharp goal from the overall improvement challenge and organized & launched just two projects aimed at achieving results. The teams involved front line employees and team leaders who were closest to the work being done. In sixty days, the teams had redesigned the source document (heretofore considered untouchable), changed the work flow, revised key procedures and instituted new tracking methods.

As a result of these straightforward actions, the backlog of late shareholder correspondence dropped from 209 per week to just 7 per week. Overtime decreased by over 100 hours per month; and the error rate decreased by 95%. With the experience gained from the first round of improvements, the teams designed follow-on projects that built on the work done in the first round.

As the case shows, progress was always possible so long as the approach was done in a way that minimized risk and managed anxiety, yet did not allow the players to engage in avoidance behavior. Punctuated approaches do just that; they enable people to experiment and to take action by lowering the threshold of anxiety to the point where they feel free to act without the fear of failure, looking stupid or trying something different (like redesigning the source document which was considered sacrosanct).

Reversing Decisions and Exiting Negative Spirals

A dinosaur frequently stems from a well-intended attempt to grow. However, as explained earlier such efforts can be misguided and will cause performance to decline. If this is the case, the management team must reverse the decision, rather than compound the mistake. It is not the time to turn toward new change programs in hopes of reconciling the decline in performance. Such actions only add complexity, cloud the picture and increase the number of variables to manage. If the management team has been committed to a flawed course of action, they simply need to stop. The reason is that once a policy or strategic decision is made, subsequent actions are taken to implement that decision. Since these actions are built on a flawed assumption, they compound the original mistake and over time grow into an integrated set of complex practices that reinforce one another and drive the organization downward in a negative spiral. It is, therefore, not enough to admit the mistake or to achieve punctuated progress. Instead, the management team needs to finish the job, commit to reversing the decision completely and extricating the organization from the flawed course of action in which it is caught. Moreover, the management team must gain insight into why it avoided and ignored the mistake or overlooked the obvious opportunity to improve performance. Finding the answer to such questions will provide the reason(s) for the avoidance behavior and/or reluctance to take advantage of an obvious improvement opportunity. It will also build the capacity of the organization to recover from mistakes in the future. Consider the following case:

A company with which I worked saw its margins erode across almost all of its product categories. The erosion occurred at the same time that sales and market share increased. I was asked to do a quick assessment to determine whether some targeted price increases or cost reductions might help. As is often the case, the findings revealed issues that were broader than expected. Here is what I learned from just a few days of interviews. Some of the cost standards had not been updated in several years. Labor rates were off by as much as 35%, and in some instances were not factored into the pricing model. No in depth margin analysis existed that allowed management to pinpoint specific causes for the erosion. Accounting produced a margin report, but it was aggregate in nature and provided little insight. Three different systems that relied on accurate cost standards had numerous mistakes and inconsistencies. These shortcomings were widely recognized and known for years. One of the systems was used by the sales organization to calculate margin, whenever they provided quotes to customers. Although the system was known to be inaccurate, quotes were, nonetheless, issued. Orders were often customized or options were added to standard products. However, since the staff did not know what the true cost of the options were, no one knew if the company lost money whenever they quoted a product that needed options. Ironically, the manager of manufacturing engineering maintained a data base that had standard hours listed for every part and every option; and every part and option had a routing that calculated the hours required as it moved through each designated operation. No one in sales or quote development knew that such a data base existed or what its potential was, save a few of the manufacturing staff. As such, no one ever asked him to enter actual performance into his data base to compare the results to the standards. Doing so would have produced a variance report at a sufficient level of detail to pinpoint the causes of margin erosion for labor and material. Because no one was aware of the data base, everyone (save the manager of manufacturing engineering) assumed that capturing actual performance was a monumental chore and, therefore, the task was to be avoided. When asked if we could add actual performance data to the standards data base, the manager explained (contrary to popular, yet uninformed opinion) that it wasn't a big deal and could be done easily. However, he made me swear that I couldn't tell anyone since he did not want to be swamped with phone calls. He explained that since the recent layoffs, he'd become increasingly protective of both his time and his staff. Other insights also came to light. The commission structure was applied inconsistently; the discount policy was often ignored to achieve sales targets; and at times sales reps circumvented the approval process to gain support for higher discounts needed to close an order.

As can be seen, the number of flawed practices that evolved within this organization was many, and stemmed from two main forces that drove the demand for better performance. First, the demand for growth prompted the decision to adopt a volume and discount strategy to increase sales & market share and to absorb burden. Had this been an installed base[15] strategy to sell parts and aftermarket services, it might have made sense; but it was not truly integrated or crafted with that strategy in mind. In fact, its parts and aftermarket functions were run pretty much independently from the core business.

Second, the industry suffered from over capacity and sagging orders. The decision to reduce fixed cost was a natural conclusion to save the business. However, the elimination of jobs was not as thoughtful or systematic as it could have been. As a result, key staff whose position it had been to maintain many of the systems and data bases, disappeared. The minute that those people left, the company started to lose margin, indirectly. When the decision was made to cut staffing levels, the intent was to keep the decline in performance from deepening further. However, the decision to increase market share and sales volume through aggressive discounting turned into a growth trap that eroded margin and triggered a series of inconsistencies and exceptions. The decision to cut fixed expenses prompted a chain of expedient actions that ultimately offset whatever cost reductions that were achieved. In-depth analysis was sorely missing; systems were no longer maintained; and, the organization acted defensively because it was afraid to tackle obvious opportunities, because it might take more time than people had available.

If this business is to improve its margins, the management team will have to reverse both decisions. The team will need to make

Exhibit 2:

Re-Aligning the Responses: Converting Insights into Guidelines and Change Practices that Work...

Four Basic Insights

- ➢ Declining performance was due to the action the management team took – not any environmental or external factors...
- ➢ Just because people know what to do, there is no guarantee that action will occur...
- ➢ Inaction and avoidance were often due to self protective and apprehensive behaviors...
- ➢ Reducing anxiety to a tolerable level was a precursor to mobilizing action and expelling a dinosaur

▼

Designing Guidelines and Change Practices that Work

- ➢ Avert the sources of a *dinosaur* and the causes of needless declines in performance...
- ➢ Confront the dinosaur and make it possible to talk openly about difficult issues...
- ➢ Expel the dinosaur by reducing anxiety to tolerable levels so people can make new choices by:
    - o Using punctuated strategies to achieve incremental gains
    - o Reversing flawed decisions and exiting negative spirals

▼

Desired Outcomes

- ➢ Capitalize on obvious opportunities to achieve huge gains
- ➢ Improve organization effectiveness (i.e., develop the ability to produce positive change & results)
- ➢ Strengthen organizational resilience (i.e., build the capacity to recover from mistakes rapidly)

new choices and replace the existing system of flawed practices with policies and practices that stop the decline in margins.

Making a Commitment to the Correct Responses and Values

The premise behind Michael Crichton's, Jurassic Park was that you could take a mosquito that was fossilized in amber millions of years ago, extract the DNA from a dinosaur's blood that was trapped in the mosquito, and then clone a living dinosaur. Despite the complexities inherent in this premise, the notion of cloning a dinosaur from a fossilized mosquito at first blush sounds plausible. Plausibility is all that managers need. They do not require the rigors of scientific discovery or the sparkle of professionally crafted change programs. Instead, they must reduce the level of anxiety and uncertainty to the point where managers feel sufficiently comfortable and confident to take action, rather than to divert accountability elsewhere. As Exhibit 2 shows, if we factor the insights gleaned from successful cases into the guidelines and change practices we employ, then we have a better chance to develop the capacity to achieve positive change and the organizational resilience needed to recover from mistakes and flawed decisions. These guidelines & practices are aligned with the behavioral realities of organizations, in contrast to responses which ignore them. In this regard, averting dinosaurs; confronting dinosaurs; and expelling dinosaurs are better adapted because they form a framework that cultivates awareness, reinforces accountability and promotes action – not a bad set of values to embrace.

Harlow B. Cohen

Summary

Confucius asked, "The way out is via the door. Why is it that no one will use this method?" One might ask the same question of managers. When the answer is clear, why do managers not take the suggested course of action? Why, instead, do they refuse to reverse a decision; demonstrate an unwillingness to replace practices that do not work with ones that do; are unwilling to take risks; use methods that overwhelm an organization or fail to produce results; or search for solutions that are external to the organization? The answer to these questions is a tautology. The reason why managers engage in avoidance behaviors is because they act defensively. Managers do not reverse decisions because they do not want to look stupid or show that they've made a mistake. They are unwilling to take risks because they fear failure, ridicule or worse. They choose to rely on outside change programs because they defer accountability and are protective of their time. Such behaviors are defense mechanisms that protect our egos, perceived frailty or psychological well-being. Responses that do not promote awareness and accountability; or that tolerate inaction are simply insufficient to meet the demands for better performance. Paradoxically, avoidance behaviors have the opposite effect that is intended. In the end, it is the avoidance that compounds the situation and erodes performance further. Taking stock of responses that are aligned with positive change, points to the way home and provides insight into what door leads to improvement and results.

Chapter Three

Averting the Sources of a Dinosaur and the Causes of Needless Declines in Performance

Many of the real dinosaurs gained competitive advantage by acquiring special traits that enabled them to be successful for millions of years. For example, the giant plant-eating sauropods such as apatosaurus, diplodocus and brachiasuarus had spoon-like teeth and gizzards that could strip and process huge quantities of conifers and cycads without chewing. These creatures could also rear back on their hind legs, use their tails for balance and feed off the tallest trees that otherwise would exceed their reach. The special design of their hip allowed these animals to perform such maneuvers. These adaptations matched up effectively with the plant life that existed during the Jurassic period. During the Cretaceous period, plants evolved into angiosperms, the flowering type of fauna we have today. Duckbills and parrot-beaked dinosaurs (e.g., Iguanodon and Triceratops) had teeth that could grind through the thick cellulose that was characteristic of the plant life at that time. They also developed broad muzzles and a head and shoulder anatomy that gave them the unique ability to feed off the ground (where the angiosperms now resided). As such, these types of dinosaurs prospered and survived while other species died out.

Each species of dinosaur became successful because it evolved traits that were aligned with its environment. Organizations are no different. Organizations, like the dinosaurs, develop success formulas and capabilities that make it possible to compete favorably. However, when a management team consciously or unwittingly: 1) Departs prematurely from the existing business model or success formula; 2) Makes non-strategic decisions to meet arbitrary growth targets; 3) Moves outside of the company's core competence to fill capacity; 4) Clutters and complicates the business with unprofitable customers, products or services; or 5) Allows individual interest to overshadow organizational welfare; then performance can decline needlessly which sets the stage for a metaphorical dinosaur in the living room. Dinosaurs can result from self inflicted organizational wounds that might exist at any level of an organization, and can vary and number as many as there were different species of the real dinosaurs. Dinosaurs are intriguing because they provide insight into how a management team enacts and interprets its environment. In this regard, the way in which a management team views and responds to the market can be of more consequence than are the external factors. It also tells us whether the management team has the capacity to acknowledge they were wrong and the courage to reverse their decision quickly before the mistake takes root. Although the executive and his/her management team may not really know or understand what factors comprise success to start, the failure to acknowledge and to reconcile an incorrect decision or course of action is what precipitates a dinosaur in the living room. Here's the paradox. Members of the management team typically knew they made a mistake or pursued the wrong course of action. It is obvious. As such, the opportunity is always present to improve performance. The opportunity always exists to reverse the decision that caused the decline in the first place. The opportunity is there to break the tie between competing elements that are pulling the organization apart. The opportunity is there to reconcile the performance shortfall; and the opportunity exists to avert a needless decline in performance; or to redirect efforts toward positive change and results.

This chapter describes five common sources of dinosaurs... I've encountered in my work with organizations. By working with the very management teams that committed the self inflicted wounds; helping them to confront the dinosaur (i.e., acknowledging the mistake without indicting anyone); and reversing the decision or changing their commitment and focus; we were able to stop the decline in performance and to return the organization to a path of positive change and outcomes.

Departing from the Success Formula or Business Model

Pundits assert that if you are not growing you are declining. Investment analysts watch securities closely to see if companies are moving in a northwest direction on the chart or if they are showing signs of decline. Geoffrey Moore asserts that capital flows toward competitive advantage and abandons competitive disadvantage[1]. Adrian Slywotzky explains that organizations migrate from "value inflow" to "value outflow"[2], if management does not maintain a constant vigil by adapting the business design to changes in customer priorities. Executives and mangers are well aware of such pressures to grow. They see it all around them; they feel it; and they hear about it daily. And more mistakes have been made in the name of growth than almost any other reason. Before anyone takes exception to this assertion, let me explain. I am not saying organizations should stand still or choose not to grow, change or adapt. This would be folly. However, there are decisions that pull an organization off course in the name of growth; depart from the success formula; abandon the original strategy when market conditions do not warrant such a shift; or simply ignore fundamental strategic principles. These decisions, many times, commit the company to a course of action that causes it to go into decline needlessly and prematurely. Once made, these decisions are hard to reverse. Rather than extricate the organization from such commitments, managers stick with their original decision, thus compounding the problem and introducing a dinosaur into the living room. Consider the following example:

A specialty retailer unwittingly found a dinosaur in its living room. The business model that the company used was to lease retail space from host stores. As such, the identity of the company resided with the host store. Each store was staffed and managed by company employees. The stores carried sufficient merchandise to accommodate consumer taste and style. Regional distribution centers located around the country supported the stores and performed light manufacturing and assembly to fill orders. Over many years the retailer developed considerable expertise and skill operating this business model. Conversely, they hadn't developed brand name recognition, employed sophisticated marketing or operated freestanding stores. This business model provided growth and excellent performance for many years until performance began to decline. What happened?

The company was publicly traded and like any publicly traded company, management was under pressure to grow. Lack of growth means that stock price stagnates and investment wanes. To spark interest and to avert this scenario, the retailer pursued acquisitions. Organic growth was not deemed sufficient to achieve the expectations of investors and analysts. When the business acquired another company, it doubled the number of stores it operated. The acquisition was presumably in the same business as the company was. Or was it? The acquired company was in distress at the time it was acquired. Management deemed the acquisition to be reasonable (maybe even a bargain), while the analysts reserved judgment to see if the retailer could demonstrate the ability to successfully acquire and integrate new businesses. Two years after the acquisition occurred, there was little progress to show and the retailer was taking on water. When the story became public, management explained that the acquisition was the primary culprit for declining performance. It also was evident that the company had not effectively integrated the new organization into the fold; however, this is only one part of the story. Although exact details are never fully available unless you are inside a company, one thing seems clear. The retailer departed from its success formula and the original business model that made it unique. Michael Porter explains that strategic positioning means performing different activities from rivals or performing similar activities in a different way[3]. By making the type of acquisition it did, the retailer abandoned its strategic positioning that differentiated itself from other retailers. As such, the company thrust itself into the world of freestanding stores, brand management and franchising – skills and competencies that the management team apparently lacked. The acquisition also required turnaround capability – again, something missing from the retailer's repertoire. Earlier in its history, the company did the same when it ventured into unfamiliar waters by buying another collection of freestanding retail stores. The acquisition became a financial disaster. The company eventually extricated itself from the situation, albeit, badly damaged by the experience. They repeated the same mistake which cost the CEO and many management staff their jobs. Although the company was able to improve performance and was on a path of positive change once again, it was eventually acquired by another firm.

This case suggests that growth efforts that ignore the existing business model/design will dilute the strategic focus, stretch both financial and human resources and compromise performance. This type of trap can be avoided if the management team thoroughly understood why it was successful in the first place. Moreover, it highlights gaps in key skill areas (i.e., turnaround skills, brand management, franchising and freestanding stores) that were not resident within the current business model because it did not require such skills. The business model simply did not include the requisite capabilities to pull off an acquisition like the one made. Such actions breed a species of dinosaur that is particularly ferocious. Dinosaurs linked to the departure of the success formula and prevailing business model can mire a management team down in the trenches for years and divert their attention from higher payoff opportunities that exist within the current model. During such times, the management team works at tinkering with the problems, rather than confront the fundamental flaw. Avenues that could yield greater returns are, therefore, eclipsed by all the activity. Even when performance returns to acceptable levels, there is little to show for the investment. And sometimes the management team becomes dinner for larger fish.

Making Non-Strategic Decisions to Meet Arbitrary Growth Targets

The South Indian Monkey trap is a hollowed out coconut chained to a stake. The hunters place rice inside the coconut that can be reached through a small hole cut into the coconut. The hole is just big enough for the monkey's hand to reach inside the coconut. The hole, however, is too small for the monkey to withdraw his fist once he closes his hand around the rice. Thus, the monkey remains captive in the trap so long as he refuses to let go of the rice. Like the monkey who refuses to let go of the rice, some business leaders latch onto the concept of growth to the exclusion of strategic focus and will not let go. In their zeal to grow, they impose arbitrary and sometimes unrealistic goals and fall prey to making non-strategic decisions that become traps for the organization.

"Forced growth – that is, growth not rooted in sound strategy – is a siren song beckoning unwary business leaders[4]. This is exactly what happened to a tier one automotive supplier hell bent on joining the ranks of the billion-dollar club. This supplier's core business provided fast-to-market vehicles to the original equipment manufacturers. Many of the projects produced relatively high margins when compared to other businesses in the automotive industry. Still, the successes and rate of growth did not satisfy ownership. They imposed artificial time frames to hasten the achievement of a billion dollars in sales. Rather than stick to the knitting, the management team, feeling under the gun and the need to please the owners, acquiesced and acquired an automotive, exterior trim business. The new acquisition manufactured extrusions. Ownership believed that at some level synergies were to be had amongst the various business units. The business consisted of multiple divisions. These divisions offered services such as engineering, product integration, design, styling and marketing. The newly acquired extrusion business was capacity driven. The original company ran assembly plants, but had no experience in continuous manufacturing. Even though, they built complete vehicles, no one had any experience in operations that converted raw material into finished goods. Many companies are sold because they are in a turnaround situation. This instance was no exception. The management team of the company had good managers and plenty of start-up experience, but had absolutely no fix-it skills. Valued members of production, quality and finance from the organization were transferred to the floundering acquisition. These folks were the company's best staff. Despite some dramatic improvements that took a year to implement, losses mounted and the banks refused to extend further credit. To support the failing enterprise, the company infused millions of dollars of cash to keep it afloat. The management team felt trapped. Exiting meant writing off significant debt – something that no one was willing to do. Another dinosaur had entered the picture!

This type of dinosaur stems from a general lack of appreciation for strategic focus and resource allocation. It also arises from impatience, unrealistic expectations and a narrow view of the world dominated solely by financial criteria. Whereas top management believes it is demonstrating good leadership by making strong demands, in effect, it precipitates unsound and non-strategic decisions. It is growth for the sake of growth. Michel Robert, author of <u>Strategy Pure and Simple</u>[5], observed similar phenomena while working with senior management teams. He discovered that when faced with unfamiliar opportunities, some management teams evaluated the opportunities by putting them through a series of filters. The most important filter was strategic fit to determine if there is congruence between the new opportunity and the overall strategic focus. When a strategic filter did not exist, the management team only assessed the financials. In such cases, if the financials looked good, the management team jumped at the chance only to discover the strategic mismatch later. These mismatches inevitably pull the entire company off course costing millions of dollars of profit and lost time. Almost twenty years earlier Tregoe and Zimmerman[6] made the same observation. They asserted, "Without congruence, the organization's strategy, its plans and its allocation of resources will simply not be aligned and the odds of its achieving its most important results will be substantially lessened." To illustrate, Tregoe and Zimmerman cite the case of a consumer products company. This firm started (like many) as an entrepreneurial venture. Despite some bumps in the road, the company grew and prospered. To continue the growth mode, senior management added new plants and the debt that went with such additions. However, the additions were made without regard to a coherent or integrated strategy. Not surprisingly, the company found itself supporting substantially different products and operating in new and unfamiliar markets. These changes proved to be very costly. At the time that such decisions were made, there were people within the organization who no doubt had doubts, but either did not express their concerns, were ignored or could not be heard. In both cases, management allowed the desire to grow and the need to please ownership to overshadow the importance of strategic focus and congruence. It is probably the single most important element of organizational success. Like departing from the business model, making non-strategic decisions to grow overlook key considerations and limitations.

Moving Outside of the Company's Core Competence to Fill Capacity

There is another dinosaur lurking inside organizations. This dinosaur has a more subtle quality. It seeks to fill unused capacity. On the surface filling capacity sounds like a good thing to do. Maybe not! To illustrate, a supplier to the utility and communications industry chose to vertically integrate its component operations because of the rigorous quality standards it demanded. It also chose to perform most work in house because many of its products were produced intermittently and in lower quantities. However, a quick review of asset efficiency and return on sales showed a gradual decline for the last six years. Their manufacturing expenses grew at an average rate of about seven percent per year while sales grew at only three percent. Nonetheless, it was business as usual. Closer scrutiny revealed that many of the assets were underutilized. For example, utilization for the stamping operations was only twelve percent. Injection molding was forty-seven percent of capacity with the hope of increasing to only sixty percent of capacity once several new products launched. Compounding operations filled only 50% of the capacity. Casting was twenty percent of capacity as were several other operations. Rather than re-evaluate the viability of a vertical integration strategy and make the decision to outsource more products, the senior management team urged sales, marketing and even the plants to search for new and even unrelated business. This decision caused the sales and marketing function to go on wild goose chases and to explore low yield markets in which the company had no expertise. Several plant managers even explored ways to fill the capacity, thereby, diverting their attention away from managing existing operations. When new business was acquired, management was pleased that utilization would increase. However, they soon learned that the new products produced more scrap, required longer set up times and often failed to achieve the needed quality standards. They unwittingly moved outside their core competencies and invited a dinosaur into their living room.

A similar problem happened to a company that painted housings for the office furniture and appliance industry. Management added another production line to accommodate forecasted growth at considerable expense. When the forecast failed to materialize and unused capacity remained high, management moved rapidly to fill the new asset with other products (i.e., computer housings and keyboards). Unfortunately, the company had no experience with the new product line and even after months of trying, still displayed little acumen. Only twelve months earlier the business unit was profitable. When asked why performance declined, each person on the management team traced the drop in profit to the addition of the new production line and the venture into different products. They explained that the new products were more labor intensive and productivity was lower than its standard products. As such, the new asset lost one million dollars per year. I asked what would happen, if we shut down the new line. The managers said (believe or not) they would lose about $200,000 per year. I suggested shutting down the production line. They balked. When I flippantly offered to unplug the assets myself to relieve them of the burden and anxiety, they explained that I could not do so because of commitments already made to new customers.

Both examples show that filling capacity is not the same as leveraging resources or core competencies. Filling capacity in reaction to low asset efficiency and high labor costs without a strategic focus and direction can compromise performance, rather than enhance it. Hamel and Prahalid[7] describe five ways to achieve resource leverage. These include actions such as: concentrating resources on key strategic goals; efficiently accumulating resources; complementing resources of one type with those of another to create higher order value; and conserving resources, as needed, and rapidly recovering resources. They explain that the concentration of resources is accomplished, in part, through *convergence,* defined as the pursuit of a single intent over a long period of time. Converging around the same goal ensures that the efforts of persons, functions and business units of the same organization do not become fragmented, as the examples above showed. The examples cited above are not isolated. During work sessions with senior managers from a variety of companies and industries, Hamel and Prahalid asked them to review the strategic plans of their companies over the past six to seven years. They found inconsistencies in direction, the markets served, the products offered, the core competencies developed and the like. In essence, the core business was changed when competitive realities did not warrant it. The managers allowed the pressure to grow to compromise the strategic direction and good business sense.

None of the examples described above sought to leverage the resources properly; nor did they have a strategic filter in place to review the decisions to broaden the asset base or to add new product lines. In the case of the supplier of hardware products to the utility and communications industries, the dinosaur in the living room was not low utilization. Instead, it was the decision to produce every component in-house, rather than outsource. As more assets were added, the financial realities sucked them into finding ways to fill capacity - a natural reaction. Unfortunately, the decision pulled them outside of their core competence. In the case of the paint business, the decision to add a new production line that was not needed was the source of the dinosaur. Once acquired, assets are hard to discard and even harder to admit the original sin. Such admissions are risky and potentially career ending moves. Still, acknowledging the mistake – not avoiding it - is the starting point. Once the dinosaur is identified, it opens the search for solutions. Conversely, ignoring the dinosaur and the decision that was made forces managers to continually feed its large appetite! And like the little shop of horrors, you can never satisfy the creature's appetite.

Cluttering & Complicating the Business with Unprofitable Customers, Products or Services...

Go to a president or general manager of a business and tell them you have a great deal for them. Explain that you will lop off two hundred or so customers and improve the bottom line. Better yet, tell them you want to eliminate some of his/her products and boost profit. Before you do so make sure you are on the ground floor of the building, or if not, pack your own parachute! It is simply counter intuitive to many managers that you can improve the profitability of a business by pruning the customer base or product line. Yet, many managers give refuge to a *Hordasaurus* in the living room that clutters and complicates the business with unprofitable customers, products and/or services. Such organizations operate under the assumption that sales of any type are good; that more is better; and that volume strategies work. Although there are, no doubt, examples to the contrary, I have yet to see a strict sales volume strategy work. For example:

In working with the same fiberglass manufacturer as described in chapter two, we discovered that the *Reinforcements* side of their business was losing seven million dollars each year despite growth in sales. This data stayed hidden until we isolated the sales and profit by asset – in these cases, furnaces. When we analyzed the customers and products produced on the *Reinforcements* furnace, we found that any account that yielded less than twenty-five percent margin lost money. And there were a considerable number of customers that needed to be fixed or exited. Up to that point, the assumption was that simply filling the asset with volume would yield a profit. Unfortunately, the assumption simply was not true.

"As good gardeners know, a bounty awaits those who prune as carefully as they plant"[8]. After years of managing turnaround companies, John Whitney found that many business units lose focus and go into decline because they are ignorant of the true profitability of customers, products and services. He explained, "... most businesses do not know the true profits of their products and services, and fewer still know the profitability of customers. Distribution and SG&A costs are rarely assigned to specific products, product groups or services. Simply put, companies have no system in place for gathering and processing such data... Managers eventually come to learn that the more they sell, the more they lose. Then they scramble to fix problems with solutions that will not contribute significantly to the company's future". To reconcile such situations, Whitney developed a *strategic renewal process*[9] that weeds out customers and/or product lines that clog the arteries of an organization by assessing them against three criteria (i.e., strategic importance, significance and profitability).

Strategic importance measures a customer's or a product's long-term contribution to a business. The initial assessment looks at what the organization does best and whether there is a match between the customer and the company's capability. In addition, the analysis evaluates the customer's health and prospect for growth as well as the welfare of the industry in which it operates. Likewise, the strategic importance of products is compared against the company's ability to be best in class; whether it can serve as a springboard for product line extensions; or if it will enhance a company's reputation or lead to new customers.

Significance refers to the current and future revenues provided by customers and products. This analysis determines the customer's quintile rank and whether the rank will improve in the near future. It also seeks to understand if the customer demands special requirements that add complexity or requires extra service. The same questions are asked of products. In many instances management discovers that a handful of customers account for the lion's share of sales and profits. Nothing is new here. Most managers understand the 80/20 rules perfectly well. They just forget these rules when budgets and incentives are involved.

An assessment of *Profitability* looks at the profit produced annually by customers and products. Customers and products are reviewed on a fully allocated basis to determine whether there is anything left for the company after the product travels the length of the system and all the customer requirements are factored. Smaller customers need as much administrative support as larger accounts do. Similarly, lower margin products need the same attention and processing as do higher priced products. This was the case with the supplier of electronic components described in the opening case of chapter one. Indirect expense climbed as more, higher maintenance customers and products were added to the mix.

The following illustration explains how one organization struggled to put a strategic filter in place like the ones that are described above:

The profitability of a manufacturer of injection molding equipment declined for five straight years. The company cluttered the landscape with too many of the wrong customers, and overcomplicated its product offering with too many highly engineered and special machines. The only saving grace was the aftermarket and parts business that was very profitable. Conversations with many managers, engineers and order processing staff surfaced concerns that top management was willing to accept almost any order. No filter was in place. More accurately, senior management ignored any filters, if they were in place. Often, the President or VP of Sales reversed decisions to reject orders that were made at lower levels. Such decisions proved to be costly, since the order generated less money than it cost to make the machine. The assumption was that anything that absorbed burden was beneficial; and since the work force was skilled, it was certainly desirable to avoid layoffs or furloughs. After a heated discussion during one of several strategic thinking sessions, the president reluctantly agreed to assess the customer base and product line. The results of the project showed that the top two hundred accounts averaged margins of 31% and comprised 35% of total profits. In contrast, the bottom two hundred customers averaged a paltry 7% margin (not even enough to cover SG&A) and accounted for only 5% of total profits. The analysis also found that more complex, highly engineered and specialized machines were being sold to the bottom quintile of customers and was not in the best interest of the company. Even more shocking was the realization that some of the most valued customers fell into the bottom category. Machines made for these "bottom feeders" as they came to be known, required on average four times the engineering hours and cost compared to the top three quintiles. In one glaring example, an order was rejected by order processing, and then later accepted by senior management despite rigorous protests. The margin for the first machine was a *negative 73%*. The argument was that the first machine might be a loss, but the orders that followed (i.e., machine #2, 3, 4, etc.) would be more profitable. The machines that followed had margins of only 8.2% - again not enough to cover SG&A. Despite the compelling evidence, the president continued the same pattern of behavior and overrode the order processing team and engineering group. He refused to accept a decision to pare the customer base or to exit any product line that was not profitable. In one instance the executive team agreed to exit an unprofitable line of machines. Later in the year a customer requested more of those machines and the president acquiesced and agreed to build them. Sales of any type were good – it absorbed burden. To acknowledge otherwise meant that the business was artificially inflated and needed to contract. Heaven forbid! Again, we see a manager driven by the fear of embarrassment, guilt or negative responses from the parent company. This failure to confront the dinosaur in the living room eventually caused management to do exactly what it did not want to do – terminate and furlough droves of employees to survive.

Allowing Individual Interest to Overshadow Organizational Welfare

One of my favorite cartoons by Gary Larson shows a stegosaurus standing at a podium illuminated by a spot light and speaking to an assembly of other dinosaurs. The caption reads, "The picture is pretty bleak gentlemen... The world's climates are changing, the mammals are taking over, and we all have the brain about the size of a walnut." The cartoon implies that there is nothing we can do to reverse the situation – it's all outside of our control. Some psychologists explain there is a key difference between people who exhibit accountability and those who do not. Someone who does not display accountability tends to explain and attribute outcomes to external factors and events that fall outside of their sphere of influence. Simply put, they do not feel that they can influence the course of events or the outcomes. In contrast, someone who shows accountability feels that events are within their grasp and believe they can influence the outcomes. Such differences have enormous implications for whether a manager takes personal responsibility for the welfare of a firm and more importantly whether they hold others accountable for their actions. After all, if you do not believe you're in control, then you might be more inclined to overlook examples where individual interest eclipses collective welfare, even in cases where it's obvious and sometimes outlandish. As shown in the aforementioned types of dinosaurs, managers avoid confronting strategic choices and obvious performance challenges. In contrast, the source of this dinosaur stems from the avoidance of confronting persons who do not act in the interest of the organization.

In one instance, a retailer of personal care products and services fell on bad times, once the founder chose to distance himself from the day-to-day business. The board agreed to search for a new CEO to lead the company out of the red and into the black. They hired a CEO who lived in a different city from the home office. The prospective CEO would only work for the retailer, if they'd allow him to commute each week. The board agreed. The CEO departed each Monday and returned each Friday, thus relegating him to a four day wonder. Once on board, he decided to hire a new CFO. The CFO he hired also lived in a different city than where the company headquarters resided. The CFO like the CEO refused to relocate. So the CEO hired the new CFO and agreed to allow him to commute each week as well. They both, coincidentally, lived in the same city and commuted together. During the first year of tenure no appreciable gains were made. The CEO spent his time trying to find a way to franchise many of the retail offices to raise cash and pay down the debt – not a bad strategy. However, this represented a low probability option that would generate cash, but would not improve the actual performance capability of the business. Doing so would require the CEO and other top executives to roll their sleeves up and make dozens of desperately needed changes. Do you know any CEO who works less than sixty hours per week and feels he/she still has enough time in the day to get the job done? The board ignored this glaring and obvious performance problem and lack of commitment. Why? Again, the answer is understandable, if we view the situation as a dilemma. Simply blaming the board gives us no insight and it is too convenient of an excuse. The owner/founder was desperate to retire and hand over the reigns to someone else and was more committed to achieving that goal than he was to optimize his selection of a CEO. Admitting that he and the board made a mistake would mean he would have to take the reigns of leadership again – something he did not want to do.

Let's look at another case. The president of an assembly business was close to retirement. One of his direct reports, echoing the sentiment of the entire staff, explained... "Let's be honest. Nothing will change here until he retires!" The rest of the staff expressed similar frustration. For example, some complained bitterly about how the president allowed the VP of Sales to run roughshod over the rest of the staff. Anytime there was a dispute between sales and order processing, engineering, marketing or manufacturing, he sided with sales. Even when the Vice President of Sales disenfranchised several regional managers who reported to him by diverting sales that rightfully belonged to the regional managers to relatives, the president ignored the indiscretions. It took two years of constant complaints from the staff and several threats to quit before he fired the VP of Sales. In another example, data surfaced during a strategic planning session that clearly showed that electric technology threatened to replace hydraulic technology. This meant that engineering should refocus their efforts to develop an electric model or that the company partner with a firm that had already developed a working model. The president's response was that electric applications would never replace hydraulic technology (a bit reminiscent of the buggy whip analogy). The new electric technology ate its way from the lower level products into the mid range and cut into the company's bread and butter product lines. Sales and marketing made a desperate plea to develop the new applications. After returning from a show where the company proved to be the only vendor without an electric model to showcase, did the president acquiesce. Unfortunately the delay forced the sales force to offer deep discounts in order to buy time until the new model was completed. In still another instance, the decision was made by the executive team to exit a line of products because margins were abysmal. The next week, immediately following the meeting, the president accepted an order for twenty of the exact same products that were discontinued.

Why bother to provide such seemingly farfetched or depressing examples of dubious leadership and decision-making? Such examples seem to reside at the far end of the spectrum. There are several reasons why the source of this dinosaur warrants mention. First, allowing individual interest to overshadow organizational welfare is an obvious and easy dinosaur to spot. It's like Tyrannosaurus Rex... everyone can identify it on sight. The behavior is front stage and in clear view. It's like watching a sports team. All the mistakes happen right on the field of play in front of thousands of spectators. The other sources of dinosaurs can be subtle or at times even invisible. These instances are not! Examples of poor management and decision making all occupy the same continuum. The only difference is that the consequences for the organization vary. Such persons cast a shadow over their organizations, business units or departments. In Built to Last[10], Collins and Porras describe myriad situations at Colgate Palmolive, Zenith, Westinghouse, Douglas Aircraft, R.J. Reynolds and Ames where a leader did irreparable harm to once great companies from which they never recuperated. For example, the authors provide an historical account of Colgate. Colgate attained over a century of growth since its inception in 1806 and was the size of Procter & Gamble at one point in its history. By the 1940's, however, Colgate fell to half its size and lost ground to its rival, P&G. Colgate Palmolive stagnated for the next four decades. The decline began when Colgate merged with Palmolive-Peet. Charles Pearce became the chief executive after decades of leadership by the Colgate brothers. Pearce appeared to be driven to grow the company into a huge conglomerate. The strategy was unsuccessful. According to Collins and Porras, Colgate's average return on sales from 1928 to 1933 declined from nine percent to four percent. He made decisions that compromised years of trust that existed between druggists, retailers and other customers by imposing unyielding terms. As a result, the druggists and other customers deserted Colgate – a blow from which the company never recovered. Finally, after years of standing on the sidelines and watching their company be destroyed, the Colgate family replaced Mr. Pearce. Thereafter, the company went through a series of unsuccessful successions of leaders.

The intent, here, is not to write another book about leadership. This is a book about organizational behavior. No different than there are principles that govern flight or laws that predict gravity, there are principles that govern organizational behavior. Our fascination with changing dysfunctional behavior is overworked and unrewarded. To quote a savvy union official I once worked with, "Don't try to teach a pig to sing. It wastes your time and annoys the pig!". This simple, yet folksy phrase has corroboration in the research findings described in <u>First Break All the Rules</u>[11]. "Simply put... the one insight we heard echoed by tens of thousands of great managers was, People don't change that much... Don't waste time trying to put in what was left out...Try to draw out what was left in... That is hard enough..." If we cannot be appreciative and build on what already exists, then we need to confront the self interest so we do not waste our time. Otherwise, we risk making this particular dinosaur a staple in the avoidance diet; and this type of diet is hard to swallow.

Explaining the Essence of a Dinosaur in the Living Room

Despite the immense diversity of the real dinosaurs, paleontologists were able to simplify and classify many species according to a few common characteristics. One defining characteristic that distinguished the dinosaurs was the skeletal structure of their hips. Some dinosaurs were classified as "bird-hipped" (e.g., the duckbills, Stegosaurus, Triceratops, Iguanodon, etc.), while others were deemed "lizard-hipped" dinosaurs (e.g., Allosaurus, Tyrannosaurs, Apatosaurus, etc.). We want to understand if the living room types of dinosaurs also share any common characteristics and determine what links them to one another.

To start, all of the dinosaurs in the living room described in this chapter explain, in part, the reasons why a decline in performance occurred. Second, the decline in performance stems from unwittingly falling into growth traps and managerial pitfalls – not from any external changes to the environment or market. Third, self protective behavior and defensiveness act as the primary impediments to reversing the slide. This avoidance behavior compounds the fundamental flaw and inhibits action from being taken. But why do managers engage in such avoidance behaviors? Are they afraid of taking risks? Are they too anxious to act? Are they too uncertain? Although the answer in many instances is yes, there is something else going on here. Every case described above involved at least two competing strategies, business models, pursuits or beliefs. For example, the *dinosaur in the living room* of the specialty retailer consisted of two incompatible business models – one that was built around a strategy aligned with free standing stores and brand identity; and another that was organized around a business design geared to host stores and host identities.

Remember the owners that imposed arbitrary growth targets on the automotive supplier? To meet the growth targets, they acquired a capacity driven extrusion business. Before the acquisition was made, the automotive supplier was a service driven, product integrator with no prior experience in continuous manufacturing. The *dinosaur in the living room* in this example introduced two competing strategies – one that had a capacity driven focus and one that was product and service driven. The strategic focus of the two entities subscribed to very different approaches that were quite simply incompatible. As a postscript, when I spoke to the CEO and inquired into why the purchase was made, he explained that he knew it was the wrong thing to do at the time, but after being urged by the owner a third time, he finally caved in and did the deal...

Reconsider the supplier to the utility and communications industry. This company chose a path of vertical integration. When they realized that many of the internal operations were underutilized, they sought to fill the capacity with unrelated products and customers. The *dinosaur in the living room* in this case stemmed from incompatible products and unrelated markets. These competing elements drew into question the real dilemma; namely, whether the company should be vertically or virtually integrated.

Let's revisit the manufacturer of injection molding machines. Analysis showed there were dramatic differences between the profitability of customers. However, top management hung steadfast to the belief that sales of any type absorbed burden. The *dinosaur in the living room,* here, was the refusal to differentiate between customers. Two competing beliefs about customers fueled the dilemma and conflict (i.e., some customers are better than others versus all customers help to absorb burden).

Last, consider the executives that showed seemingly poor decision-making ability. In the case of the less than full time CEO, the *dinosaur in the living room* was due to a competition between self-interest and organizational welfare. Retirement took precedent over the company's well being. The same competing priority applies to the president of the tier one assembly company. He either did not want to take any action that would taint his last days in office or he was waiting to cash out with a severance package. Even the historical case of Colgate hints that the Colgate brothers did not want to come out of retirement and that Pearce, the CEO of Palmolive, saw his name in lights as he tried to grow the company into a huge conglomerate.

The common characteristic that links many of the dinosaurs in the living room together is the reluctance or avoidance to break the tie between two or more incompatible elements. To repeat, whenever two or more competing strategies, business models, pursuits, beliefs or commitments co-exist within the same organization or business unit, and such incompatible elements are not reconciled, then you have a good chance for producing a dinosaur in the living room. The strategic focus splits and the day-to-day activities splinter. Under such conditions, performance declines because resources and people become thin. Organizations do not do well, when its members must support multiple agendas; especially ones that compete. Imagine an umpire who after a pitch does not call a ball or strike. The game stalls and cannot proceed. It is no different for an organization. When management does not make the call and allows ambiguity to seep in, it taints the key tasks of the company like a drop of ink in water. Human beings cannot absorb undue complexity or tolerate ambiguity for prolonged periods and still be successful running a business; especially when there is less time in which to do more work with fewer resources as discussed in chapter two.

Kegan and Lahey[12] provide additional insight into why people inexplicably know what to do, but seem unable to act despite recognition that action is exactly what is needed. They explain, "Resistance to change does not reflect opposition, nor is it merely a result of inertia. Instead, even as they hold a sincere commitment to change, many people are unwittingly applying productive energy toward a hidden competing commitment. The resulting dynamic equilibrium stalls the effort in what looks like resistance, but is in fact a kind of personal immunity to change"[13]. Recall the plant manager of the fiberglass facility who would not rehire the direct labor he had just laid off earlier in the year. He knew he should rehire more labor for the forming room, but had a competing commitment of not losing face with the union and employees. A more recent example involved a President of a stamping operation. After five years of success and double-digit profit improvement, the company stalled and began to decline. The management team members surrounding him were long time associates whom he worked with when he was a plant manager at one of the many stamping facilities. He pulled many of the management team from his plant into the corporate office. Unfortunately, few of them knew how to make the transition and failed to perform to higher expectations. Despite tremendous pressure from his superiors to change out the staff, he attributed their concerns to the economy and external events. He spent hours justifying his decisions and referenced past performance. He could not change due to a competing commitment of loyalty to his staff and the realization that many of them could not make the step up. This competing commitment ultimately proved to be his undoing and he was asked to retire.

Although such examples are individual in nature, the same dynamic applies at group and organizational levels. As Kegan and Lahey state, "Although competing commitments... tend to be deeply personal, groups are just as susceptible as individuals to the dynamics of immunity to change. Teams, departments and even companies, as a whole, can fall prey to inner contradictions that protect them from significant changes they may genuinely strive for"[14].

On the surface, it appears that the dinosaur in the living room is another way of chastising managers for their inability to make a decision. Not so! Contrary to conventional wisdom, change is not always the right course to take. The origin of a dinosaur in the living room may stem from making ill advised decisions. In many of the examples, performance declined after a management team made the decision to grow in ways that contradicted established strategic principles. When managers ignore such principles, they eventually rediscover what researchers have known for decades; that is, a sharp focus and clear strategic positioning are key to competitive advantage; strategic tradeoffs prevent companies from becoming all things to all people and from diluting resources; and, an organization's activities need to, at minimum, be consistent or reinforcing of one another to form a more cohesive system[15].

What does all this mean? It means that the genetic code that produces a dinosaur in the living room is two fold in nature. First, the source of a dinosaur in the living room may grow from misguided, resource allocation decisions that introduce two or more competing elements into the system that cause performance to decline needlessly. Second, the dinosaur in the living room takes root and expands into other rooms, when the original decision is known to be flawed, yet it is ignored or avoided due to fear, anxiety or apprehension. This means that there are two closely linked dynamics going on in parallel– one that is organizational in nature; and one that is psychological. At the surface, we find competing choices that have a direct impact on how resources are allocated; how strategies are deployed; how organizations are structured; and how performance is impacted. These types of decisions are often treated in the literature as sterile and devoid of emotion, but they are anything but… To the contrary, they are very personal and emotionally charged. Consequently, a psychological tug-of-war underlies many organizational changes between self protection and safety; and taking a risk by making a flawed decision public or explicit which could possibly invite a negative response (something to be avoided). It is this ambivalence that all of us experience, when we must choose between actions that might heighten anxiety or expose us to perceived risk; and inaction that keeps us safe and maintains anxiety at a manageable level (even though we know intellectually that something in the organization is amiss).

Summary

Orson Scott Card exclaimed, "Some people hear a lie when told the truth[16]". It takes courage to listen to the truth and not deny it. It takes courage to acknowledge the reason for declining performance. It takes more courage to reverse or reconcile a misguided decision. Taking responsibility for results, rather than engaging in avoidance behaviors is likewise, not easy. However, as explained, this is not a case where a company must engage in radical change efforts, revamp the whole organization to stay alive or redesign its entire business model to respond to industry-wide changes. Instead, confronting the dinosaur in the living room arises from known opportunities with known solutions using existing resources. Five sources of dinosaurs grew from observation and work with a broad spectrum of companies. These sources appear to share several common characteristics that might not be so obvious. First, many of the dinosaurs that plague a business have a split personality or are two headed. They originate from decisions that contradict well-established strategic principles and introduce two or more competing strategies, business models, beliefs or pursuits. Whereas, the initial reason for declining performance stems from: a) departing from the original business model; b) making non-strategic decisions to meet arbitrary growth targets; c) moving outside of core competencies to fill capacity; d) cluttering and complicating the business with unprofitable customers, products or services; and e) overlooking individual performance problems; the compounding reason for decline is acting defensively which prevents the management team from breaking the tie between two or more dueling elements.

Chapter Four

Confront the Dinosaur in the Living Room: Making It Possible to Talk Openly About Difficult Issues…

For nearly a century, scientists presumed that dinosaurs were cold-blooded and resembled reptiles more so than warm-blooded mammals. It was not until Armand de Ricqles and Robert Bakker challenged this assumption in the 1970's that efforts to disprove the cold-blooded theory took shape. During the course of their search to prove the warm blooded hypothesis, Bakker uncovered research conducted in the 1930's that provided compelling evidence that the dinosaurs might, indeed, be warm blooded. In addition, he found another extensive body of data that included comprehensive studies that showed that cross sections of dinosaur bone looked more like mammals than reptiles. These studies dated back to the 1950's, but likewise, remained obscure. Bakker explained that despite such evidence, it appeared that "…orthodoxy suffocated dissent"… and therefore, "no one paid much attention to the data…"[1] To overcome such orthodoxy, Bakker directly challenged the prevailing norm by resurrecting old data to support his new assertions. Only by building a compelling case backed by overwhelming data gleaned from decades of pre-existing work, was Bakker able to combat years of dogma and denial, and advance his assertion and theory.

Like the paleontologists just described, managers must find ways to rediscover what they already know and to challenge the avoidance behaviors that hide huge performance gains. There are three levers that managers can pull to confront a dinosaur in the living room, uncover the performance opportunity and to galvanize action and positive change: These include: 1) infusing urgency 2) legitimizing debate; and 3) putting the lie to the dinosaur.

Harlow B. Cohen

Infuse Urgency

The first step in confronting a dinosaur in the living room is to infuse urgency into the situation. Infusing urgency awakens the dinosaur and jolts the lethargy that surrounds it. To infuse urgency management must raise the stakes, demand results and immediacy and take away the air cover. This must be done in a way that does not indict prior performance or blame persons. For example, the group president described in the opening case of chapter one, infused urgency by charging the general manager with doubling profit in a matter of just six months. He mandated that the management team mobilize and make whatever changes would achieve a ten percent pre-tax profit. In so doing, he raised the stakes and demanded immediate results. By asking the team what it would do to achieve the goal, he took away the air cover and any excuses. Too many executives and managers ask why performance declined. In response, they get all sorts of creative explanations and excuses that do absolutely nothing for confronting the dinosaur and achieving concrete results. In fact, the explanation serves as a proxy for action. Since the performance shortfall was explained, there's no need to change – the explanation supplants action. As my old mentor explained, "Don't ask questions that you do not want the answers to…"

The combination of a strong, clear-cut demand and an insistence on showing results in a relatively short time frame aroused the management team to action. Demand for results and short-term time frames are two sides of the same coin that are key to infusing urgency. Robert Schaffer has long known, advocated and urged managers to design change projects that yield results using rapid cycle breakthroughs. He explains, "By selecting a goal that is clearly urgent and setting a first step that can be accomplished in a short time, some of the energizing forces... can be stimulated in a disciplined, controlled fashion"[2]. The president cited in the opening case did exactly that; he let the management team know that low performance was not an option any longer. Instead, he replaced complacency with urgency; and exchanged passivity with immediate action and results.

John Kotter asserts that establishing a sense of urgency is the first of eight-steps in leading a change effort[3]. Kotter believes that managers grossly underestimate "the enormity of the task..." despite a general recognition that most change efforts fail. As Kotter explains, "... sooner or later, no matter how hard they push, no matter how much they threaten, if many do not feel the same sense of urgency, the momentum for change will probably die far short of the finish line". If normal change efforts fail, imagine what is needed to confront a dinosaur that represents an opportunity that evaded attention and avoided confrontation for months or years.

The CEO of a supplier to the appliance industry discovered similar lessons. Although the company existed for many years and enjoyed moderate and sometime stellar success, the return on sales inched steadily downward for five straight years. The dinosaur housed in the living room included a growing level of fixed assets. Despite this trend, no one was particularly concerned. After all, the company was not losing any money. Despite many offers to buy the business, management resisted any attempts at being acquired. Because the company was private, its performance was not open to public scrutiny or the press. The management team prided itself on its commitment to its employees; and a fierce dedication to maintaining its current practices. All of these factors added to a very complacent environment. Complacency often acts as an incubator for developing a dinosaur in the living room. Complacency numbs the senses, makes it possible for managers to collude with one another to avoid confrontation and causes the organization to go into a deep sleep.

To reverse the trend and to overcome the apparent avoidance mechanisms, the CEO instituted several changes to heighten the urgency and to raise performance expectations. To begin, he set forth a goal to double revenue and profit over the next seven years. By setting a goal to double the size of the company, the CEO drew a line in the sand that was easy to measure and to understand. There was no vagueness. Unlike some goals that assert the need to become world class or the market leader, this demand was concrete and unequivocal. The goal made it clear that organic growth by itself would be insufficient. As Collins and Porras explain,[4] "All companies have goals, but there is a huge difference between merely having a goal and becoming committed to a huge, daunting challenge – like a big mountain to climb". Collins and Porras found that visionary companies – the ones that lasted fifty years or more - commanded extraordinary recognition, outperformed their entire industry and often used big hairy audacious goals[5] (termed BHAG's) to stimulate progress. Companies like Boeing, P&G, 3M and Hewlett Packard frequently used such mechanisms to spark urgency and to achieve dramatic results. In fourteen out of eighteen cases, the authors of <u>Built to Last</u> found BHAG's in greater evidence than in any of the comparison companies. And the comparison companies were not poor performers. In many instances they lasted as long as the visionary companies, but could not muster the same level of accomplishments, as did the visionary companies. For example, Jack Welch put forth the challenge to become number one or two in every market that GE served. He divested or sold those businesses that failed to achieve that goal. In so doing, he infused urgency, mobilized people and released dramatic, untapped potential that catapulted GE to even higher performance.

Second, the CEO decided to take the company public and to register with the SEC. By taking the company public, the CEO drew back the curtain behind which the management team was hiding and exposed its flaws, warts and dinosaurs. Like the Wizard of Oz exclaimed when Toto pulled back the drape, "Don't pay attention to that man behind the curtain". Going public removed any veils that protected the business from public scrutiny, shareholder review or an analyst's evaluation. The air cover was now gone even though some acted as if nothing changed. Going public also reinforced the initial goal to double the size and profit of the company. Failure to accomplish this assertion would be greeted harshly by shareholders.

Managers hide or avoid the challenges they face, even when it holds huge potential to improve performance. For example, I recently had occasion to work with an organization that developed an innovative and well-thought out proposal to outsource an entire assembly operation from one of its customers at a cost savings of millions of dollars per year. According to the president, the top managers for the customer acknowledged that the logic and proposal made sense, but decided against doing the deal. Why? Recently, the customer had closed one plant and built another brand new facility with much greater capacity. Doing the deal meant that the customer would have to write off significant dollars. Even so, the deal proposed by the supplier was still economically feasible. Unfortunately, the top two executives were the same guys that decided to build the new plant. The feeling was that the investment community would greet such a decision with harshness (no doubt). Writing off the investment in the short term would prevent the achievement of the proposed profits; so they acted self protectively and nixed the proposal at the expense of the company and the eventual benefit to the shareholders.

In contrast, General Electric, under Jack Welch's leadership, sought to practice open book management. He introduced mechanisms like the Workout process to eliminate wasteful practices, streamline work processes and to transform the culture into one where people could be candid. As Welch expressed, " Look reality in the eye and don't flinch! Without facing reality, it was impossible to stay competitive and impossible to win. The winners won because they assessed their opponent's strengths and the playing field accurately. The losers fell by the wayside because they stuck their heads in the sand"[6]. The Workout process forced senior managers to make decisions on the spot in response to improvement ideas put forth in the Town Meetings in front of an assembly of 30-70 persons; sometimes including one's boss seated behind the decision maker. Such activities significantly heightened urgency that was missing from the system, compressed the decision making process and prevented managers from using delay as a tactic for avoiding or ignoring long-standing opportunities.

Some managers find fault with infusing urgency saying that you cannot sustain a feverish pitch or operate in a crisis mode forever because of the burnout factor. Perhaps, but my experience suggests that what burns people out is not urgency. Instead, people burn out when their level of frustration rises at a steeper rate than their learning does; or gives way to boredom born out of frustration. And nothing adds more to frustration than avoiding obvious changes that people know will make a difference.

Legitimize Debate

A second lever that managers can pull to confront the dinosaur... is to *legitimize debate*. Legitimizing debate means that senior managers must move the improvement opportunity or competing priorities facing the organization from backstage to front stage. Discussion must shift from closed to open forums. Sunshine laws apply here, not private discourse that can't be questioned or scrutinized. Managers must also turn implied expression into explicit dialogue so that people can hear what is being said. Talk and chatter tends to be nebulous and general and, therefore, by definition cannot be accurate or specific. To counteract such vagaries, managers should produce data to back up opinions. Would any of us take medication based on an opinion that a drug is safe? Then why accept an opinion on face value that could be the very pill or poison that alters the well being of a company? Toward this end, it is wise to validate assumptions and the stakeholders who hold those assumptions. In this way, it is easier to map disparities that are due to functional/departmental preferences as compared to differences that are more substantive and do not subscribe to political squabbles. Last, managers should push for closure to long standing debates. Dinosaurs love unfinished business. It gives them a respite in lazy lagoons where the water can support their enormous weight. Drain the swamp and make them move to one side or the other, rather than straddle the fence.

One of the insidious aspects of a dinosaur in the living room is that people do not want to take the time to resolve the debate or to break the tie between competing priorities or strategies. They implicitly know that it will take time and energy – something they do not have, believe they do not have, are reluctant to acknowledge or simply use as another form of avoidance. Accordingly, managers simply avert the challenge and live with the duality that is killing the organization.

This was the case with one company. Three longstanding dinosaurs stood steadfast in the organization, remained unresolved and served as obstacles to change, growth and improvement. The first debate centered on whether to rationalize manufacturing facilities. The contention was that efficiencies would more than offset the one time costs incurred for the move. Arguments to the contrary contended that rationalizing facilities could be risky. The second debate focused on whether it made sense to offer a broader range of products to meet more customer needs. Some explained doing so was a source of competitive advantage, whereas, others believed it added undue complexity and cost and diluted the focus. The last debate raised the question of whether the company should operate as a global firm with specialized centers of manufacturing excellence, or remain divided into localized domestic and international operations. Many advocated a local focus to accommodate a nationalistic bent in Europe and South America, while others felt the company could not afford the luxury of duplicate cost structures.

These debates lasted years and took on the characteristic of a submarine, submerging from sight for prolonged periods and then surfacing for a short time before disappearing again. Whenever, the CEO broached any of the three topics, all he got was silence. His staff did not want to stir the pot or run the risk of going to war with other functions. Frustrated by the lack of closure and declining performance, he charged the Vice President of Finance with the task of tackling the three debates. The CEO explained that he wanted the data and ammunition he needed to make decisions on all three questions. He further explained that this activity would be a test of the VP of Finance's flexibility and openness to change. There would be no more excuses. Armed with nothing more than the fear of what might happen, if he failed to provide the CEO with what was asked for, the VP promptly formed three task forces. Each task force had to clarify the assumptions underlying the debate they were to resolve. Each task force had to build a compelling case for action backed by data that either validated or invalidated the assumptions surrounding the debate. Each task force had to be cross-functional in nature to ensure diversity of opinion. Each task force had to offer clear-cut recommendations to the CEO and his executive team. Each team had to make improvements that became obvious, did not require capital or were simply no-brainers. And they had no more than 90 days to complete the assignment.

Let's look at the first debate and what the team uncovered. Their task was to determine whether or not to rationalize manufacturing facilities, thus creating one plant dedicated to related products and processes; and the other one dedicated to a different set of similar products and technologies. The team found a strong rationale for making the change. For example, they found that 50% of the products made at the western facility would fit on existing machines in the east. The eastern plant at the time was only 50% utilized and, therefore, could achieve significant labor savings by using existing crews. Duplicate and on-hand inventories would decline as would set ups and change over costs. More importantly, they discovered that moving one set of related products east to the sister plant freed up over 50,000 square foot of space. Freeing up the space in the western plant made it possible to streamline the order to ship cycle, and to eliminate the need for outside warehousing and non-value added material transfers. Such a change would provide an estimated three million dollars of reduced production costs and a fifty percent decrease in lead-time. Even without the benefits of the streamlining effort, the rationalization process showed that the company could glean $1.5 million annually versus a one-time cost of $1 million. The data were all there for the picking.

If the data were there all along, what enabled the debate to rage for so long and prevented closure? The answer lay hidden in the way the system worked. To start, the plants operated as cost, rather than profit centers. Thus, any operations that absorbed burden were welcomed, not questioned. Over time habits of accretion cluttered the plants with a variety of activities and work cells. Second, the plant manager of the western operation was a long-term employee and wielded considerable influence. Last, the company operated as highly autonomous silos. Data that was resident in one functional silo was not accessible to other functions. As such, the puzzle pieces remained scattered or left in a jumble in the box. When a cross functional team dumped all the puzzle pieces on the table, it was not long before a clear picture emerged and the debate ended.

The second debate called into question whether a highly diverse product offering was the right direction in which to move. As one can imagine, the opinion varied depending on the department with which you chatted. For example, sales and marketing felt it was essential to customer retention and satisfaction to present a broad offering of products. They also felt there should be sufficient safety stock to cover urgent demands that customers might need. Manufacturing and inventory control felt very differently. A broad product line played havoc with scheduling, changeovers and inventory turns. To resolve the debate and to get the ball rolling,

The Dinosaur in the Living Room

the team ran several reports. The reports showed that there were 12,000 part numbers listed on the system, but only about one third had any sales activity over the last three years. A closer analysis revealed that of 150 product families, only 41 accounted for 90% of the sales. The remaining 109 product families comprised just 10% of sales. Whereas sales for the top 41 products families grew at a compounded growth rate of 5% per year for three straight years, the bottom 109 product families declined by 42% during the same time frame. As might be expected, some of these products had two to three years worth of inventory in stock. Still another breakthrough achieved by the team was the decision to allocate fully absorbed cost (minus manufacturing overhead expense) at the product level. Prior to taking this action, the company had never allocated full costs at the product level. This action blew the cover off the debate. When fully absorbed costs were applied, the profit margins of those product families that were suspect declined by almost 25%. Many of the products dropped significantly in margin contribution and others showed losses. If the customers would not accept price increases; if manufacturing could not improve operational efficiency; or if engineering could not redesign the product, then the company would have to exit selected products and jettison the related cost.

What was underlying this debate? Why was this issue able to avoid closure? What were people avoiding? Some debates are clever ways that us humans use when we are scared to venture forward. By keeping a debate afloat, we evade action, tests and perceived risks; or sustain organizational myths. The product proliferation debate obfuscated a more daunting task. The core business showed signs of aging. It was running out of steam and many within the company knew it. Industry consolidation, fierce competition and intense pricing pressure simply accelerated the process. To offset these countervailing forces, Sales & Marketing introduced product line extensions to see which ones would stick. These attempts did in fact add sales, but the sales were insignificant, non-strategic or unprofitable. The proliferation added dramatic complexity, cluttered the manufacturing sites and made it more difficult to be efficient. We know from research that although product line extensions may account for the majority of growth in sales, such extensions contribute to profits at a much lower level[7]. As such, it does little to extend the life of a core business or to defend effectively against rivals. Sales and marketing were out of bullets and did not know what to do differently. Legitimizing this debate forced closure; showed that management needed to take a different tact; and revealed the myth that more sales were always a good thing to do.

The last dilemma facing the company was whether or not to form into global specialty operations or to continue down the path of localized, regional operations. At first, the team thought that it must solicit the opinions of multiple constituents. They soon found that each stakeholder held a different viewpoint and suggested a different solution. For example, many of the European operations explained that unlike the United States, companies in Europe were quite nationalistic and sensitive to outsourcing to other countries. Other stakeholders felt that tariffs and shipping would offset any gains achieved by forming global manufacturing centers. Still others felt that going global would enable plants to fill their capacity and achieve higher profit. Faced with such diversity, the team worried it might never finish the task. To overcome the dilemma posed by the myriad opinions, they decided to replace the subjective viewpoints with data. To get started, they reviewed the utilization of every operation across the entire company. Much to their dismay, they found that utilization was woefully low in many operations. For example, in one plant location the up time of milling was only 17%. In another plant, utilization of the injection molding operation averaged less than 50%. They uncovered data that showed that the company outsourced forged components to suppliers at hundreds of thousands of dollars in excess of what their sister plant charged. Duplicate inventories totaled in the millions. Significant opportunities surfaced to reduce freight and handling. It also became possible to consolidate platforms, standardize parts and to combine sizes and product variations. The options and course of action were now evident with few exceptions.

As described in the other examples, data were readily available. Nothing new was invented. No innovations were introduced. No one was fired or hired. The team simply used existing data to draw clear-cut conclusions. Once done, the decisions became obvious. For example, they decided to consolidate the manufacture of metal fabrication into a single plant that would act as the global supplier to the entire company. They took the same action for injection molding and extrusions. It was a bloodless coupe. The old business model assumed that plants should act like independent fiefdoms. After all, that was how its founder operated and he was successful. However, over time many of the products turned into commodities. It was no longer cost effective to continue the same practices. As the exercise showed, confronting the dinosaur in this instance meant letting go of practices and a model that was less effective. Managers oftentimes do not like to acknowledge obvious decisions for fear that they might look stupid. Guess what?

It is virtually impossible in organizational life to advocate a position, strategy or direction without triggering a contradictory position, strategy or direction. That's the fun of running a business.

There is no one best way. Since the basic nature of a dinosaur in the living room consists of at least two competing elements, legitimizing a debate forces a company to articulate and acknowledge the basic proposition (like the three outlined above) and to examine it from at least two perspectives – usually pro and con. The debate can also be broken into more than two perspectives to represent the various stakeholders so that all the views are in the open. The different stakeholders must present supportive arguments and data to create a compelling case for or against the basic proposal. The point of this type of debate is not to declare a winner. Instead, the intent is to cultivate awareness, foster accountability and to give expression to issues that remain unspoken. In this way, a bridge is built between the implied and explicit; between assumption and fact; and between spoken and unspoken assertions.

Put the Lie to the Dinosaur

Putting the lie to the dinosaur is somewhat like the little boy in the fairy tail of the emperor's new clothes who blurted out, "The emperor is naked. He's not wearing any clothes". Putting the lie to the dinosaur in many ways requires the candor and innocence of children, but the understanding of an adult. There are three activities that managers can do to put the lie to the dinosaur and to achieve huge gains in performance.

One tactic is to make explicit, the assumptions that underpin the decline in performance. Often, managers hold faulty assumptions or harbor armchair theories of how organizations work. These theories fail to appreciate key differences between organizations and ignore key success factors that are still very much alive. Such assumptions may also be untested or have little or no validity.

A second tactic for putting the lie to the dinosaur is to untangle twisted thoughts[8] that color and distort the dialogue surrounding the dinosaur. It is critical to listen closely to the way that managers and employees talk. Hidden in the dialogue are the clues that provide insight into what faulty assumptions and thoughts are keeping a lock on the huge potential that exists.

Last, putting the lie to the dinosaur may require managers to surface and highlight any competing agendas that sustain never ending debates. Many times it is not outright resistance that prevents progress, but a dilemma where managers are uncertain, too anxious or equally committed to different courses of actions that are incompatible.

Making Assumptions Explicit

Sources of dinosaurs (like the ones described in chapter three) may explain why an organization experiences a needless decline in performance. Such dinosaurs, however, are often complex and difficult to sort through once they've taken root. The reason why they are so difficult to overcome is that they are built on assumptions. Assumptions are the building blocks of organizational behavior. Assumptions guide managers in a given direction and determine their actions. However, assumptions are typically invisible or hard to access, yet have tremendous force to shape behavior and actions. They reside just below eye level. Ask an executive to elaborate on what his or her assumptions are that underpin a course of action or strategy. Be prepared for word salad. Unless we can make the assumptions explicit and gain an understanding of what the dinosaur and avoidance behaviors are based on, it is difficult to lend insight into the needed changes.

Consider the following example. A division of a building materials supply company experienced a decline in productivity for two straight years. The Vice President, General Manager was tearing his hair out because he was unable to make any progress. After listening to the VP/GM describe the situation, we suspected that there was more than one assumption operating that explained the lack of progress. Rather than ask the managers what their assumptions or theories were about the shortfall in performance, we instead (as suggested by Mitroff[9]) focused on key differences between various stakeholders who were involved in the process. There proved to be three key stakeholders involved (i.e., manufacturing, production control and sales/customer service). In talking with the various groups, it became clear that they possessed different rationales and untested assumptions that allegedly explained the decline in performance. For example, the manufacturing superintendent explained that the reason why performance declined was due to the constant changes to the production schedule dictated by sales and customer service. To prove his point, he developed a color-coded, floor-to-ceiling diagram that resembled a spectra graph. The graph showed the scheduling changes and the weekly output. On the surface it looked like a compelling argument. However, there was no proof to show that a statistical correlation really existed between the changes in schedule and the output. He was convinced that unless the number of changes to the schedule decreased, there was no way that any gains in performance were possible.

In contrast, production control, the department responsible for changing the schedule, expressed a different view. They felt that scheduling changes had some effect on output, but did not explain the whole picture. They assumed that since each shift was tracked individually, rather than as a total team that a degree of unhealthy competition existed. They observed that each shift sub-optimized the performance of other shifts to meet their numbers. They cited many instances of how one shift achieved their required output at the expense of another shift. For example, one shift ran their equipment non-stop and ignored scheduled maintenance rebuilds. This meant that the next shift was forced to shut down to do the required maintenance on the equipment and, therefore, experienced additional downtime as a result. Over time each shift was caught in a zero sum game and sub-optimized the overall performance.

Last, sales and customer service insisted that the company had no choice, but to respond to customer needs and changing priorities, and that it was manufacturing's headache to figure out how to do it. This position assumed that there was no choice in the matter, and if it meant lower performance, it was better than a loss in sales or poor customer satisfaction ratings.

Let's examine the various assumptions, implied or otherwise. The first assumption expressed by manufacturing was that performance was driven by external factors; namely, changes made to the production schedule by customers. Whereas this assumption was seen as crucial to output by manufacturing, it was not a certainty.

The second assumption expressed by production control assumed that performance was driven by internal factors and systems (i.e., the performance and tracking system). As such, they believed that the performance system shaped people's behavior and, therefore you got what you measured. The production control department's assumption was viewed by them as important to output, but as in the first case was not proven to be valid.

The third assumption asserted by sales and customer service was that productivity was less important than meeting customer demands. They assumed that manufacturing and production control should embrace this belief and accommodate whatever changes the customer wanted; otherwise the company would lose the account. Whereas this assumption was important to sales and customer service, it really was not germane to the question of productivity; nor was it certain that customer needs actually impacted productivity, negatively.

Mitroff and Mason[10] suggest that such complex issues and key differences be plotted to show their relative position in comparison to two key factors – importance and certainty. The first assumption advanced by manufacturing was important to performance, but uncertain. The second assumption expressed by production control was also important to performance, yet uncertain. The third assumption offered by sales and customer service was not important to performance and uncertain, and consequently was discarded. To determine the certainty of both assumptions, we gained agreement from senior management to freeze the schedule for two weeks. Sales and customer service were free to pick the product mix, but once selected, it could not change. Output improved, but only by two percentage points. Next, we changed the tracking system from monitoring individual shifts to total daily and weekly production. Output jumped 7 percentage points. We agreed to freeze the schedule for the balance of the month until the numbers showed less variation. Once output stabilized, we gradually introduced more scheduling changes until it was no different than before the project had started. Just as many changes to the schedule were being introduced as before. Nonetheless, productivity remained high regardless of what scheduling changes were thrown at manufacturing.

The example illustrates that just because people view their assumptions as important does not necessarily mean that the assumptions are valid. In fact, the example showed that manufacturing's assumption only explained a small portion of the variance in output. Production control, on the other hand, seemed to pinpoint the key issue in the system; that being, the performance and tracking system reinforced the wrong behaviors and unwittingly fostered actions that allowed *individual interest to overshadow organizational welfare* (our fifth source of a dinosaur in the living room). When proven that the scheduling changes were an insignificant factor in predicting output, the game changed, output increased and the total system benefited.

Untangling Twisted Thinking

In many ways, confronting a dinosaur in the living room is like therapy. The idea behind therapy is to establish co-dependence between the patient and therapist, work with the patient in ways that allow them to overcome their avoidance and/or defensiveness and to then enact changes to one's behavior. This is done by providing the person with sufficient support/concern so as to increase his/her tolerance for anxiety. Confronting the dinosaur in the living room, likewise, seeks to increase the tolerance for anxiety to the point where people are willing to act and, thus, overcome defensive behaviors. It involves getting a management team to acknowledge and articulate what they already know and to take action; even if the action is modest. How do managers and executives overcome avoidance and defensiveness? The answer resides in two types of anxiety connected to change - learning anxiety and survival anxiety. The famed psychologist, Edgar Schein, noted for working with Korean prisoner of war veterans who were brainwashed, explained; "The basic principle is that learning only happens when survival anxiety is greater than learning anxiety. Learning anxiety comes from being afraid to try something new... or that we might look stupid... or that we will have to part from old habits that once worked. Survival anxiety is the realization that in order to survive and make it, you must change"[11]. However, acting passively may still be seen as a valued route to survival (i.e., don't rock the boat and keep your head down). Raising the level of survival anxiety seems easier for managers to do. Managers simply have to threaten or coerce people and change occurs. However, raising the level of survival anxiety exacts compliance and passivity, not commitment. Passivity sustains a dinosaur in the living room and makes it harder to overcome avoidance because no one wants to take any perceived risks. The key, then, is to reduce the level of *learning anxiety* which admittedly, is harder.

To tackle learning anxiety, managers must understand that the anxiety is often based on cognitive distortion[12]. Cognitive distortion used, here, is one of several terms for twisted thinking. Examples of twisted thoughts might include all or nothing thinking, jumping to conclusions (i.e., mind reading and fortune telling), disqualifying the positive, magnification or minimization, overgeneralization, mental filtering, labeling and blaming[13]. All humans engage in these types of distortions. Such thoughts color perceptions and cause us to behave in counter productive ways. The behaviors that prevent a management team from correcting its mistake once discovered is sometimes due to twisted thoughts that have little or no basis in

The Dinosaur in the Living Room

reality. These thoughts keep the organization stuck in the doldrums. Consider the following example:

Interviews conducted with a cross section of managers revealed that an automotive supplier had become too asset intensive and had too much overhead. As such, the company was not producing enough cash to fund future growth despite relatively healthy margins. Many of the staff felt that senior management succumbed to habits of accretion, and as such, almost every new product required additional capital and new equipment. For example, the asset to sales ratio was 50% compared to a benchmark of 15%. Depreciation expense (calculated as a percentage of the cost of sales) was 17% compared to a benchmark of just 4%. These same habits caused the business to become dramatically overstaffed given its size and nature. For example, from 2003 to 2004, payroll increased by almost two million dollars exclusive of benefits. Rather than acknowledge these two obvious opportunities, the general manager launched a series of over 60 improvement projects that he reviewed every day; and he instructed the sales force and quote development office to diversify into new and different markets.

Excited by the findings and the prospect of converting a multi-million dollar loss into a huge gain, we presented our case for action to the General Manager. Not surprisingly, we got serious push back during the presentation. For example, he minimized the negative impact that the assets and depreciation cost had on the profitability of the business. He explained that the assets were already paid for by the customers and did not understand our concern. He mitigated the benchmark data by asking if we had collected data from any of the direct competition. And he asserted that he had already come to the same conclusion regarding the staffing levels long ago.

Each of these responses highlights the anxiety connected to the proposed changes and the implied evaluation of the GM's performance. Each of the expressions was an example of twisted thinking and apprehension. Only on the surface did some statements sound plausible. For instance, the assertion that the assets were already paid for sounds plausible on the surface and might cause one to ignore the evidence. In reality, this is an example of *minimization*[14]. According to Dr. Burns, minimization is like taking a pair of binoculars and turning them backwards so that what you are looking at appears to shrink in size and importance[15]. The distortion in this type of thinking is sometimes designed to find evidence to support some pet hypothesis – namely that assets are always a good thing because they build the value of a business. In this case, the General Manager lessened the role that depreciation cost played in the declining performance of his business. He convinced himself that the cost of the assets was built into the piece price of the products. Unfortunately, he ignored the fact that the actual equipment remained on his balance sheet and that he, in fact, paid the depreciation cost for every asset, every year for the life of the product. He also assumed that the sales volume achieved during the life cycle of the product would meet the forecast. If the sales volume fell short of expectations, then the cost of the equipment might not be covered; and then he'd be in a no win argument with the customer.

His question about the benchmark data is an example of a *mental filter*[16]. When managers use a mental filter, they pick out one negative detail from the whole in an effort to discount the overall value. Think about his statement. We just shared industry data and he asked if we had any information on his direct competitors. Why? If the competition was at the same level of performance, then it was okay and he could ignore the data. Unfortunately, his business was the one that was losing money.

Last, his assertion that he already knew that the business was overstaffed is an example of *jumping to conclusions*[17]. Jumping to conclusions assumes that you can read someone else's mind and, therefore, there's no need to validate or to inquire further into what you heard. For example, was the business over staffed by 10% or 50%? Was the organization overstaffed in the hourly or salaried ranks or both? Was the ratio of direct to indirect employees too high? The GM never questioned the assertion, glossed over the detail, preempted his learning and concluded he already knew.

It is not uncommon to hear distortions or twisted thoughts. We hear them all the time. One manager with whom we worked stated that his work force was too old to adapt to a lean manufacturing approach and, therefore, it would never work. The comment is an example of *all or nothing thinking*[18]. All or nothing thinking is the tendency to paint the world in black and white terms. Hardly anything organizes neatly into absolute dichotomies. Will all the people over age fifty be unable to adapt? Could fifty percent of those workers who were over the age of forty adapt; or only those workers with facial hair? The statement is also an example of *jumping to conclusions* or *fortune telling*. What if the management team does a really excellent job of communicating and training? Is it a forgone conclusion that the lean implementation will still be a failure?

What's the point? The point is that you cannot talk people out of their anxieties, defensiveness and twisted thoughts. Rather than fight such behaviors, which will only strengthen people's resolve and the belief that their thoughts are valid, a better tact is to acknowledge the concerns, determine what type of distortion is being expressed and find ways to talk back to them. By talking back to the thoughts explicitly, you are quite literally putting the lie to the dinosaur. For example, when the General Manger of the automotive supplier stated that the assets were already paid for, we gave credence to the possibility. We asked him to explain what he meant. He explained that the cost of the capital equipment was built into the piece price charged to the customer. We then asked if the assets still remained on his balance sheet and whether he was paying the depreciation cost shown on the profit and loss statement. He acknowledged that, indeed, he was. However, when we asked if the sales volume had materialized, he became quite animated and accused one of the customers of not making good on their forecast or promises. We then asked what the impact of that one customer was, and the GM explained it would cost him hundreds of thousands of dollars of unabsorbed expense. By this point in the conversation, it had become obvious that the strategy he had employed was quite vulnerable. There was no need to push the point further, since we had given expression to the issue.

Next, we gave legitimacy to his assertion that he already knew that the business was overstaffed. We asked when he had become aware of this realization. He said that he was aware of this fact for at least the last six months. We asked him to estimate by how many people he was overstaffed. He stated that he was not certain of the numbers, but that he planned to reduce headcount by about a million dollars. However, he was not certain of the date when such changes would be implemented. We then asked whether the figures included the six staff that had been hired in the last month. He went silent and searched for a spot on the floor to look at…

Let's revisit the example where the manager in charge asserted that the workforce was too old to adapt. We again treated the statement as possible and real. We asked what the definition of older was. In an age of political correctness that is not an easy answer. He explained that he didn't really mean older from an age perspective. What he really meant to say was length of service. We asked what his definition of length of service was. Frustrated and worried that the questions might undermine his argument, he explained that there were blocks of employees that were set in their ways and that these people would not be receptive to any attempts at change. Undaunted by his claims, we asked if any changes had been implemented despite such resistance and what the outcome was. He explained that there were, indeed, instances where change occurred despite the resistance. We then asked him to identify the ingredients that were present in the successful change efforts that were not there for the unsuccessful ones. We found that age and length of service were not one of the variables anymore than were employees who blocked attempts at change.

It is difficult, if not impossible to confront a dinosaur in the living room that is pulling an organization down, if we do not understand what is preventing people from acting. As explained in chapter one, managers create artificial barriers and limitations that prevent them from creating positive change. Managers' failure to act, rather than their failure while acting are the primary challenge[19]. In part, twisted thinking and distorted rationales serve as the excuses and explanations for inaction. As shown in the aforementioned examples, such thoughts and rationales are connected to people's anxieties. And such thoughts and rationales typically stay locked inside someone's head or behind closed doors. By forcing internal dialogue into the open, we can hear what is actually being said. We can make the anxieties explicit by listening closely and patiently. We can examine and challenge what is said; and we can determine whether the thought has a basis in reality or is simply a distortion that has little or no basis. Tackling the dinosaur at the interpersonal and emotional level erodes the grip that twisted or unfounded thoughts have on "learning anxiety" and the self protectiveness that suppresses the potential that remains hidden.

Reconciling Competing Agendas

As explained earlier, it is not always resistance that gets in the way of confronting the dinosaur. Instead, it is incompatible agendas and/or competing commitments[20]. Recall the definition from chapter three that Kegan and Lahey present. They explained, "...resistance to change does not (always) reflect opposition, nor is it merely a result of inertia. Instead, even as managers hold a sincere commitment to change, many people are unwittingly applying productive energy toward a hidden competing commitment[21]." In chapter three, I explained that the essence of the dinosaur in the living room stems from the failure to break the tie between competing strategies, business models, beliefs or commitments. At times, a management team will support a dual agenda that is inherently conflicted. They suspect the elements are incompatible or cancel each other out, but do nothing to reconcile them. How, then, do managers resolve the dilemma and reconcile the contradiction? The answer to the question is straightforward. To start, managers need to remind themselves that there is no such thing as a free lunch. To get something we want, we must give up something else we might also want. Economics teaches us that there is an *opportunity cost* connected to pursuing a given course of action. The opportunity cost is whatever must be given up to obtain a goal. Managers should, thus, opt for that choice which has the lower opportunity cost, when the elements are in competition. For example, in some of the cases cited earlier, a management team decided to tradeoff sales volume for profit by pruning the customer base. Others chose to tradeoff selling lower margin products in order to create the capacity to sell more, higher margin products. Still others elected to free up engineering time to work on new product development, rather than spend effort on order processing. The economic principle of *comparative advantage* instructs us to make a tradeoff between those activities that we are best at doing (i.e., has the lower opportunity cost) and to let others perform activities at which they are best at doing. These principles provide insight into another way that managers can confront the dinosaur in the living room and to set the stage for action – *reconcile competing agendas and force a tradeoff.*

To reconcile an agenda and to force a tradeoff, it is necessary to first paint a black and white picture and to place the competing issues on opposite sides of the fence. This means that there can be no shades of gray. In this way, the competing factors can be examined more closely, and the opportunity cost can be calculated to determine what the competing commitment is costing the organization. After polarizing the issue and evaluating the competing agenda, the next step is to force a tradeoff and to make a choice. This action will take tremendous courage. However, failure to make such a tradeoff will relegate the organization to a hazy no man's land and ensure that the dinosaur remains steadfast in your living room. I found that before a manager will act they must feel sufficiently convinced that he/she has a reasonable assurance of success. Let's illustrate the approach:

A company that produced lighting products watched its economic indicators decline for four straight years even though the economy was favorable. Return on sales dropped from 12% to 7%. Profit growth steadily declined year over year. The asset to sales ratio also showed a negative trend. The asset base increased by several million dollars, added to the drag on profits and needed more sales just to stay even with where it was four years ago. The installed base of product in the field compared to new product sales grew to an order of magnitude of 42:1. As a result, order quantities and dollars per order steadily declined. The company prided itself on customer service and satisfaction. Over time, however, the business unwittingly found that this ironclad commitment to customers produced a two-headed creature – one that was high volume continuous manufacturing; and another that was low lot size intermittent production. Unfortunately, both types of production co-existed within the same plants and ran on the same equipment. As one can imagine, set up costs sky-rocketed, production runs shortened and manufacturing expense climbed on average by 7% per year as high volume lines were interrupted to fill smaller order quantities.

To respond to the decline in performance, the VP of Manufacturing and the VP of Sales & Marketing along with their staff convened a meeting. They reviewed an analysis of the orders that showed that margins of the twenty highest volume products had dropped by almost 14% concurrent with the rise in low quantity orders. Additional reports and analyses revealed similar findings. It was soon clear that the two types of manufacturing were incompatible. Further discussion exposed another *competing commitment*[22] that sales and marketing displayed. They expressed an unwillingness to let go of the smaller orders because they feared that the business would turn into a commodity driven enterprise – something that already had happened. They also feared that they might not be able to find replacement business to compensate for the increase in the installed base of product that was in the field.

They knew they had to move downstream toward the customer and search for outsourcing opportunities, but were unsure how to do so. Accordingly, they stayed committed to any order that looked like a special in hopes that it might turn into a high flier one day. Virtually none of their efforts turned into significant, strategic or new revenue streams. The paradox was that they expended most of their time shepherding and attending to the larger volume products and customers.

Rather than exit the entire low lot size, intermittent production business, several creative options emerged to force a much-needed tradeoff. First, they decided to separate the two businesses. They admitted that the *opportunity cost* connected to running a high volume business along side a specials business was simply too great. The high volume, continuous manufacturing operation remained independent, but was no longer interrupted by intermittent special orders. As such, margins on higher volume products rose almost immediately. Low lot size, special orders were moved to Mexico in order to reduce the overhead and burden that existed in the high volume plants. Many of the products were run once or twice per year and then stocked and shipped north at regular intervals. It was not long before the people running the specials business realized that there were other manufacturers that sought to rid themselves of interruptions and intermittent production. This strategy allowed them to sell not only to customers, but also to competition. Rivals wanted to augment their product offerings, but were unwilling to compromise high volume operations. This strategy created the chance to acquire outsourced assembly operations that customers no longer wanted to perform. They had inadvertently discovered a way to move downstream to the customer and to acquire much higher margin service related growth opportunities.

Alfred North Whitehead exclaimed, " In formal logic, a contradiction is the signal of defeat; but in the evolution of real knowledge it marks the first step in progress towards a victory". Reconciling competing agendas and commitments embraces contradiction, but then takes a step towards resolving it, thus setting the stage for action and ridding the organization of the dinosaur that suppresses performance. As the above case illustrates, reconciling competing elements and forcing a tradeoff concedes that a management team cannot have its cake and eat it too. Failure to choose is not an option. As Michael Porter explained, " ... a strategic position is not sustainable unless there are tradeoffs with other positions. Trade-offs occur when activities are incompatible. Simply put, a tradeoff means that more of one thing necessitates less of another. An airline can choose to serve meals – adding cost and slowing turnaround time... or it can choose not to, but it cannot do both without bearing major inefficiencies[23]".

In the movie, *Indiana Jones & The Last Crusade*, the villain, in hopes of achieving immortality, drinks from what he believes to be the chalice from which Jesus once drank. Before he drinks, the ancient knight guarding the chalice urges the villain to choose wisely from the vast number of cups on the table. The villain chooses the wrong chalice and turns into dust in a matter of seconds. Upon seeing the demise of the villain, the knight quips, "He did not choose wisely". Faced with never ending dilemmas, competing agendas and contradictory commitments, managers must consistently choose and do so wisely, or suffer a similar fate; only the villain is a dinosaur that straddles the fence and blocks the organization from getting to the other side.

Summary

Confronting the dinosaur in the living room (i.e., making it possible to talk openly about anxiety provoking issues) is one set of activities that can be taken to achieve positive change and large performance gains. The intent is to reveal and highlight the avoidance behaviors and defensiveness that prevent organizations and its members from responding effectively to the causes of poor performance. Confronting the dinosaur encourages truthfulness about what impedes progress. It searches for the obvious and does not discount the ordinary, if it applies. This tactic seeks to expose the behaviors for what they truly are. The idea is to blow the cover off of the avoidance behaviors that stand in the way; and to form the foundation needed to galvanize action. At this point in the process, the issue is recognition, acceptance of accountability and mobilization more so than solutions. Solutions come shortly, thereafter.

Infusing urgency, legitimizing debate and putting the lie to the dinosaur are three specific ways in which managers can look at their behavior and the behavior of the organization in general; and to be honest about what it needs to do to improve performance or to reverse the decline. Each of these tactics subsumes a range of techniques for combating avoidance behaviors and anxiety that otherwise would enable garden-variety dinosaurs to sip tea, seated undisturbed in the living room. For example, *raising the stakes, demanding results and taking away air cover* awaken the organization and jolt its complacency. *Moving dialogue from closed to open forums, backing up opinions with data, highlighting differences between stakeholders and bringing closure to longstanding debates* alert the organization that change is afoot; that candor and openness are valued; that perceptions must be validated with concrete data; and that targeting low hanging fruit and tackling the obvious are okay. *Making assumptions explicit, untangling twisted thoughts and reconciling competing agendas* challenge faulty beliefs, erode defensiveness; sharpen the focus; and force tradeoffs between incompatible activities that rob the organization of profitable opportunities, confuse employees and consume critical resources.

In the *Wizard of Oz,* Dorothy believed that she had to endure many trials and challenges before she could go home to Kansas. She eventually discovered that she could have gone home at anytime. Like Dorothy, managers may find that the answers they seek may already be in front of them, once they learn to put a stop to the avoidance behaviors by exposing the behavior for what it is; and by identifying the hidden issues that need to be dealt with…

Chapter Five

Expelling the Dinosaur from the Living Room: Using Punctuated Strategies to Achieve Incremental Gains

Darwin's theory of evolution dominated thought for most of the twentieth century and strongly suggested that changes in species were ongoing and continuous. As such, many believed that dinosaurs constantly evolved in response to the many changes that occurred to their habitat. How else could they live for so many millions of years? In 1972, Eldredge and Gould[1] advanced a revolutionary new theory called punctuated equilibrium. The theory suggested that species were not evolving continuously at all. Instead, adaptation and evolution for the most part remained static. When evolution did occur, however, it happened suddenly in bursts, and typically within isolated, smaller populations; hence the term punctuated. This theory explains why it is so difficult to find missing links. Applying this theory to the evolution of dinosaurs, Dr. Bakker visited sites that were rich in layers of fossil remains and that spanned many millenniums. He discovered that, indeed, skeletons of dinosaurs, like Brontosaurus, remained unchanged for millions of years despite many dramatic shifts in climate and the environment. He also found that when changes did occur they were "... major jumps forward in quick evolutionary spurts[2]" and were disconnected from the main body of the primary population. The validation of "punctuated equilibrium" as a viable theory of how evolution works set the stage for understanding how certain species remain unchanged for eons, whereas, others evolved more frequently.

We need to take a page from the theory of *punctuated equilibrium*. When managers realize that they need to tackle the obvious; or recognize that they made a decision that triggered a decline in performance (as described in chapter three); or finally decide to confront the dinosaur in the living room; they need to attack the challenge in measured ways and on a smaller scale. This means managers should use *punctuated strategies and incremental interventions–* actions that break the tie and foster quick bursts in performance, yet are smaller in scope and scale to manage the risk to the organization and to keep anxiety at a manageable pitch. There are several reasons why using punctuated strategies are preferable and more effective than large-scale, total systems change.

Reasons for Using a Punctuated Approach

Contrary to conventional wisdom and despite claims to the contrary, large scale, complex and abstract change efforts are high-risk endeavors that tend not to produce results[3]. As described in chapter one, studies show that such change efforts have very low chances of success, about twenty to thirty percent. When I use the term large scale, complex change efforts, I speak of those efforts that seek comprehensive and organization wide transformation, renewal or change. These types of efforts tend to engage in massive training, reorganization, human resource interventions or abstractions such as cultural change, empowerment, learning and the like. In contrast, punctuated strategies such as small or short-term wins, kaizen events and breakthrough projects have a higher batting average and produce tangible and measurable results. More importantly, punctuated approaches aim at breaking the tie between competing strategies/priorities, whereas company wide, abstract or complex activities stall the very decision that will mobilize action and unleash potential; that is, unless such a large scale approach can generate a multitude of smaller, punctuated changes (e.g., Appreciative Inquiry, Workout, etc.).

Second, although the prevailing logic advocates a total systems approach, the actual outcome of many large-scale change efforts are nothing more than the rearrangement of the existing structure chart, installation of a system or delivery of a comprehensive training program. As Ashkenas explains, "Boxes are moved around... teams are ceremoniously launched, layers are removed, support services are consolidated or distributed, but the fundamental performance capacity of the organization remains unchanged[4]". In contrast, performance capacity is built by taking small steps that develop skill. Studies performed by McKinsey & Company showed that sustained high growth companies achieved progress by maintaining a continuous pipeline of business building initiatives[5]. The mechanism by which growth was achieved was done one step at a time. As the authors explain, "Executives... face two big problems: market uncertainty and gaps in their skills and assets... successful growers typically address these problems by taking not bold leaps, but a series of measured steps. Each step takes them a little closer to their ultimate goal... and adds capability... When these growers look back on what they achieved, they see not a chaotic zigzag pattern, but a distinctive staircase... While few single steps are dramatic, when linked as a staircase of sequential growth they create dramatic results[6]".

Additional support for a punctuated approach comes from Beer, Eisenstadt and Spector. They conducted a study of six companies that tried to implement large-scale transformation or renewal efforts[7]. The study involved hundreds of interviews conducted over five years involving twenty-six plants and divisions. The results of the study ultimately compared successful to unsuccessful change attempts and uncovered several unconventional findings. For example, one key finding highlighted the importance of "starting corporate renewal by targeting small, isolated peripheral operations rather than large central ones..." Another finding discovered that, "...change efforts that begin by creating corporate programs to alter the culture or the management of people in the firm is inherently flawed even when supported by top management". Other data revealed that, "formal organizational structure and systems are the last things an organization should change when seeking renewal – not the first, as many managers assume". These studies corroborate my own experience in working with management teams that must compensate for the presence of a dinosaur once discovered; and to improve performance or to reverse a declining pattern. I've found that too many large-scale change efforts confuse building infrastructure with generating results[8]. Rather than target short term, incremental outcomes, such efforts focus on intermediate or abstract variables. Managers mistake implementing a materials planning system for reducing inventory; they mistake resolving conflict for shortening lead-time; or they mistake empowering front line employees for improving labor efficiency. Structure, systems, measurements, rewards, training, team building, empowerment, learning and dozens more comprise a company's infrastructure. Many managers assume that if they put enough of the right support elements in place, results will spring forth like a fountain from a rock in the middle of a desert. Nothing could be further from the truth. All that happens is that the complexity and enormity of the task overwhelms the staff. Support elements are key to sustaining results once achieved. However, they do not on their own produce outcomes because such elements are intermediate, not causal. The moment that managers start down the infrastructure path, they commit to a lengthy process that is not geared toward resolving any of the competing elements that are the source of a dinosaur in the living room. Eventually, these efforts run out of steam with little or no results to sustain the effort because the dinosaur and inherent dilemma remain untouched.

Third, like the patterns found in evolution, organizations need some stability. Organizations that sustain themselves year after year are reasonably well attuned and adapted to the current conditions and their respective customer base. It means that the business model and strategic proposition work. The prevailing literature would have us believe that organizations must constantly be in flux in a never-ending effort to adapt to a dynamic flood of environmental changes. No one disputes the need to change at times. But constant change can be just as detrimental as no change. As seen in chapter three, when managers departed prematurely from the original success formula or made non-strategic decisions to grow or cluttered the organization with non-strategic products and customers, the organization went into decline. The evolution was faked and artificial. No true adaptation or improvement occurred. All that happened was that the organization lost valuable time and diverted attention from accumulating capital that could foster productive growth. Using a punctuated approach provides folks with familiar signposts, while change is implemented. In this way, the organization is not turned into tossed salad, and managers can reduce the risks associated with all or nothing strategies, thus, keeping dangerous use it or lose it mentalities at bay.

Fourth, managers do not always know what actions will compensate for a dinosaur in the living room or positively affect the desired outcomes. Dinosaurs that exist in an organization typically languish unchallenged and unabated for months or even years. Much of what we think will work is untested or speculative. Until we take action and commit to a selected path, we do not know what we might bump into... Strategies do not always play out exactly as we think they might and managers simply cannot conceive of every possibility. Armed with the first hand experience gained from taking punctuated actions, it is easier to shape a longer-term blueprint of the future. It is more prudent to stick one's toe in the water to check the temperature before diving in or getting scalded.

Last, proposed change efforts spark higher levels of anxiety. People do not perform well, if anxiety is too high. When confronted with stressful challenges, many managers revert to familiar patterns that worked before. For example, pilots who learned to fly aircraft in Europe, after World War II, learned to turn their aircraft up side down whenever they got into trouble, because the planes ejected downward. When the same pilots transferred to the United States and flew planes that ejected upwards, several were killed. Confronted by an emergency the pilots turned the planes upside down and ejected into the ground[9]. Lucky for us, managing an organization does not have the same risks as flying a jet does. Still, the pattern of behavior is similar. Managers may rely on old behaviors that once worked, despite repeated failures in hopes that the practices will somehow work again. Using a punctuated approach allows people to practice and correct mistakes once discovered. So long as the effort is incremental and lower risk, it is okay to make mistakes. This tack keeps anxiety lower and gives people the chance to learn what works and what does not.

Using Alternative Strategies that Subscribe to a Punctuated Approach

If managers ignore the reasons just described, they will find it difficult to dislodge a dinosaur from the living room, capitalize on obvious opportunities or to reverse a decline in performance. Comprehensive approaches take too long to unfold and fail to break the tie between the competing elements that caused performance to decline in the first place. Conversely, managers that integrate the reasons described above will find that a punctuated approach is more effective. Of greater importance is the realization that dinosaurs are surrounded by months or even years of avoidance behaviors and defensive reasoning. Punctuated strategies are designed to minimize anxiety and manage risk; thereby reducing defensiveness. Table 5.1 summarizes the main reasons why traditional approaches to change will not expel a dinosaur; and offers five punctuated tactics that a manager can use to implement positive change:

Build Capability by Terracing the Improvement Effort

Even after a management team comes to grips with the obvious changes facing an organization; and even after a compelling case for action is made; it is still difficult to take the first step, because people may simply lack the skills or capacity to effect the required changes. As such, they do not want to look stupid. To provide the right type of positive signals, change should follow a developmental path no different than managers do in their careers. Why? Because managers and other key players do not gain exposure to the types of jobs or assignments that teach all the skills needed to reconcile the five sources that breed dinosaurs (i.e., departing prematurely from the existing business model/success formula; making non-strategic decisions to meet arbitrary growth targets; moving outside of the company's core competence to fill capacity; cluttering and complicating the business with unprofitable customers, products or services; or allowing individual interest to overshadow organizational welfare). No one is born knowing how to fix such decisions once a dinosaur takes root. The skills have to be acquired.

Table 5.1 Comparative Strategies…

Reasons Why Traditional Change Efforts Will Not Expel a Dinosaur…	Using Punctuated Strategies to Expel a Dinosaur…
❑ Large-scale, complex or abstract change efforts exceed the capacity of the organization to absorb the changes… ❑ Too many change efforts focus energy on support elements to the exclusion of results… ❑ Large-scale change efforts tend to ignore the stable elements of an organization… ❑ It is not always clear what actions will work or not work… ❑ Change efforts often spark higher levels of anxiety and defensiveness…	❑ Build capability by terracing the improvement effort… ❑ Work with existing limitations until confidence builds… ❑ Search for incremental actions that will trigger a chain reaction… ❑ Find more than one way to win… ❑ Make effective tradeoffs…

The Dinosaur in the Living Room

One way to build capacity and skill is to terrace a series of progressively more ambitious improvements. *Terracing* forces managers to view their organization as a series of developmental steps to climb. Each step holds increasingly more potential. However, each successive improvement requires greater skill and coordination. Organizations that are unable to reconcile performance shortfalls at a departmental or unit level are unlikely to tackle declining performance at an organizational level. People must show dexterity at each successive level and develop competency before expanding their field of vision. Performing a cross-functional project demands more skill than conducting a limited departmental project. Performing an organization-wide transformation or managing an entire value chain demands an even broader range of skills and criteria than managing a cross functional process. None of this should be a surprise to veteran managers. Building capability is no different than going through an apprenticeship before one becomes a master craftsman or a black belt. Such skills are earned by tackling progressively more difficult tasks and trials. Since it is highly unlikely that a company can effectively move from point A to point D, it is simpler to take measured steps and to put building blocks into place. This is exactly why a punctuated strategy is preferred. It is a less daunting task to build capacity in stages than all at once. Consider the following example:

Several years ago I worked with a company whose operations showed signs of weakening allegedly due to industry consolidation and market changes. However, when I spoke with the individual management team members, I heard a very different story. Rather than blame the economy or market for a multi-million dollar sales decline over a three year time frame, they instead pointed to the sales and marketing function as the culprit. Many of the executives strongly felt that the drop in sales was directly due to the lack of marketing talent and expertise more so than market forces. Some went so far as to say that only a sales organization existed despite the presence of marketing staff. Others claimed that sales and marketing had no incentive to perform, rested on their laurels from years past and should be put onto a variable compensation plan. Further analysis showed that of twenty new products released by marketing over the past few years, eight were canceled after expending one full man year of product development time. Only two of the twenty projects generated 92% of the total revenue of the remaining twelve. Although this information was common knowledge and data based anecdotes swirled throughout the organization, no action was taken. One reason for the inaction was that the sales function controlled and buffered the other functions from critical customer and key account information. As such, the president had real concerns that any sweeping action aimed at marketing might result in a worse scenario. In working with the sales and marketing organization, it became clear that the managers were resistant to outside help. The sales and marketing function was unwilling to listen to any feedback. They felt that the noise in the system was due to a lack of knowledge of what was really happening in the market. They attributed the entire shortfall to consolidation and market changes.

Here was a great example of a dinosaur... Performance was in decline. The need to improve was compelling; data existed to provide insight into the sources of the decline; there was a difference of opinion between functions; and the dialogue was not yet public or open to debate. It was clear that many of the senior managers did not want to confront sales and marketing directly, cause conflict, run the risk of being proven wrong or losing face.

The Dinosaur in the Living Room

Rather than directly confront marketing and sales, the president decided to move downstream to manufacturing and to improve operations. Work processes, cycle times, material and information flow were streamlined. With the advent of shorter cycle times, the sales function was forced to shift from using forecasts to providing actual customer demand for each product line. This action required that sales and marketing be trained. Order processing and customer service decentralized and relocated from the corporate office to the plants to eliminate duplication. Scrap and defects per million reduced and labor efficiency improved. As the manufacturing effort took hold, profits rose and the company moved out of the red and into the black again.

Buoyed by the success and momentum gained in manufacturing, the president next turned his attention to improving the engineering and product development function. To get started, engineering focused its energy on creating a process with which to assess new projects and new product development efforts. In the past, engineering performed whatever projects that sales and marketing handed to them. Without an assessment process to buffer the engineering activity, priorities were shuffled constantly. This delayed the completion of many projects and elongated the product development effort. The benefit to the company became clear. They would be able to determine which projects represented the best opportunity for the corporation as a whole, and engineering could plan and allocate its engineers, accordingly. Sales and marketing balked at the idea of being constrained by an administrative or bureaucratic procedure due to the time it might take. In particular, they railed at the prospect that someone other than themselves would decide which projects to pursue. In reaction, engineering collaborated with IT and found a way to automate the project/product assessment process and to apply more sophisticated tools such as the internal rate of return and net present value. In addition, a corporate committee was formed with the president's approval. The committee's task was to review proposed projects and to reinforce the shift from unilateral decision making to cross functional and collaborative participation. Cycle time for capital allocation and decision making dropped to days, rather than weeks and sometimes months. Excuses evaporated and participation broadened to include multiple functions. These modest shifts provided managers with the chance to learn, apply more sophisticated tools and to strengthen engineering and manufacturing. It did not take long before the screening process singled out higher payoff projects from ones of lesser value. Once the new assessment process was up and running, engineering launched another effort to streamline its product development cycle time and to enhance its program management skills. In this way, engineering could directly impact sales by decreasing the time it took to get new products to market. In doing so, engineering also increased its capacity to absorb new projects, thus putting pressure on marketing to deliver product plans and new customer/market opportunities that merited their attention. Otherwise, engineering would need to reduce its staffing levels.

It seems odd that a company would tackle everything except marketing given the circumstances and sentiments. In fact, they might be accused of avoidance. However, the president's actions significantly strengthened two key functions (i.e., manufacturing and engineering), improved overall profit and achieved a higher degree of operational excellence. Given the current situation, if the president had not terraced the improvement process starting with manufacturing and engineering, he may have put his company in a

The Dinosaur in the Living Room

position where gains in sales and marketing could not be supported operationally. At times, organizations plow forward, venture into new arenas, crank up the growth engine and even diversify before they have a strong foundation in place. In such instances, growth may very well occur, but it is not long before management is pulled back to address operational problems and issues of customer dissatisfaction. When an organization can assert that it is operationally excellent, it can focus on penetrating existing accounts, targeting new customers, opening additional markets or diversifying. In this regard, the president showed a great deal of courage, political savvy and planning. He terraced the reversal process into three distinct, yet related segments, holding marketing to last. In addition, each successive improvement served to *punctuate* incremental adjustments that the marketing function needed to make in response to the growing capability of manufacturing and engineering. For example, in response to manufacturing's ability to shorten lead times, marketing had to shift from forecasts to real customer demand. This incremental change revealed the true value and priority of certain customers. Participating in a cross functional product committee forced the marketing department to work with other functions. They had to assess and justify new projects using more sophisticated tools and methods before any engineering resources were assigned. Decentralizing customer service enabled manufacturing to come into direct contact with the customer for the first time and to break the lock that marketing had previously possessed. Thus, the systems nature of an organization enables changes made on a small scale to have a ripple effect on the larger organization without necessarily changing everything all at once!

GE's Workout process is a more heralded example of how a company incrementally increased its performance capacity and the ability to absorb change, despite massive layoffs. To compensate for the loss of thousands of jobs, GE launched a Workout process to extract non-value-added work practices from its system. In the early days, the Workout process focused on eliminating reports, layers of approval, meetings, policies and unnecessary procedures. Such efforts were limited in scope and focused largely on administrative waste. Welch next challenged the company to expand its field of vision and to attack core work processes, not just administrative tasks. As a result, the second iteration of Workout involved process mapping and cut across multiple functions and entire business units. Lead and cycle times evaporated. Once the company showed dexterity to effect changes with its internal processes, management again enlarged the field of vision to include suppliers and customers that produced even greater gains. Each iteration of Workout built additional capability, introduced new tools/methods and expanded the capacity to absorb more change. The Workout process spanned many years and was terraced into stages, thereby, moving gradually from a limited administrative focus to a total value chain perspective.

In Built to Last: Successful Habits of Visionary Companies[10], Collins and Porras found that a comparison of the best companies to those that fell just behind focused energies on *building a better clock rather than simply telling time*. These companies invested effort in the "...company itself as the ultimate creation". To quote, " It's not just the building of any random clock; it's building a particular type of clock. Although the shapes, sizes, mechanisms, styles, ages and other attributes of the ticking clocks vary across visionary companies, we found that they share an underlying set of fundamental characteristics. The important thing to keep in mind is that once you make the shift from time telling to clock building, most of what's required to build a visionary company can be learned[11]". Whether one builds a growth staircase as suggested by McKinsey; or terraces progressively more challenging tasks, as the example above illustrates; or takes a single tool like Workout and applies it across a variety of organizational boundaries; the strategy is the same – build capabilities continuously and incrementally so when the time comes that your organization experiences decline (and it will), the management team has the skill and resilience to compensate.

Work with Existing Limitations Until Confidence Builds...

Before my father died, he used to say, "The nicest thing about hitting your head against a brick wall is how good it feels when you stop". Sometimes, it is easier to work with the existing limitations of an organization than it is to swim upstream, develop the skill base or to expand the performance capacity. This type of incremental strategy is used to compensate for a dinosaur in the living room by generating momentum and getting the ball rolling. It is also useful when there is enough ambivalence to prevent progress or to draw the chances of success into doubt. In such instances, managers must discover what people are able and willing to do.

Some years ago I worked with a vision care retailer. A feud existed between different stakeholders as to why sales lagged in some regions and stores, yet excelled in others. One group asserted that store sales would improve, if more resources were invested in the OD (i.e., doctor of optometry). Advocates of the OD theory felt that effective OD's bred patient loyalty and the stores directly derived product sales from such relationships. Conversely, others believed that sales would improve and the OD would benefit, if better merchandising and advertising existed. Feeling trapped between these two competing views created a dilemma for the president. Depending on which view dominated made a dramatic difference on how resources would be allocated and where the emphasis would be applied. Should the company invest in new equipment for the OD or use its capital to redesign and merchandize stores? Should the company offer more convenient hours to customers or broaden the product offering? To resolve these questions, I worked with the president to conduct an analysis to determine if, indeed, there was any relationship between the actions taken by the OD and store and regional sales. The investment of time required from the key players was minimal, since all that was needed was data that was already available and easily retrieved.

The findings showed strong statistical relationships between higher store sales and the number of exams performed by the OD. It also showed positive correlations between higher store sales and customer convenience, as measured by the total hours of coverage offered by the OD and the hours worked by the OD after 6PM. The study also showed that the OD tended to perform more eye exams in higher performing regions; and that in these regions the OD offered broader coverage and more convenient hours than lower performing regions did. It was now clear that the OD played a more significant role in achieving higher sales performance at both the store and regional level. Further analysis showed that higher performing stores averaged $300,000 additional sales dollars than lower performing stores did. The sample only included 46 stores. Many more stores existed.

Although the sales opportunity was enormous, the scope of the change effort was equally large. The president was, therefore, reluctant to make such sweeping changes. Even though he knew

The Dinosaur in the Living Room

such changes could impact sales by millions of dollars, he was unsure how others (especially the OD) would react and what resistance he might encounter. Rather than launch a large scale, far reaching change in policy, we targeted a handful of lower performing stores in a few regions that were willing to test out the findings and had nothing to lose. We, thus, shaped a punctuated series of changes that resembled a terrace or staircase. Each action sequenced the introduction of policy changes such as growing the number of eye exams, extending the hours of coverage and increasing the total hours worked. Each action was also expected to improve sales performance. And each action was staggered so there was no overlap and people had time to adjust and react. By using a punctuated and incremental approach, we were able to advance the agenda, achieve incremental progress and work with the limitations that were inherent in the debate. Rather than declare a winner and loser based on the findings of the study, the president simply implemented the changes to only those stores and regions that were willing to try something new.

Here was an example where the debate would dampen any attempt at launching a broad based policy change... Pursuing a strategy of this nature was not feasible given the difference of opinion and unwillingness to break the tie. A dinosaur of this type remains steadfast in the living room because the key players have struck a balance of power that enabled both factions to co-exist. Unfortunately, this system of implied détente prevents the organization from realizing even greater potential. Bob Schaffer in his book, <u>High Impact Consulting</u>[12], explains that there are many situations (like the one described above) where the scope and pace of an intervention are not matched to what the client is ready, willing and able to do. Schaffer advocates that a thorough up front assessment of readiness is key to successful implementation and achieving results. The assessment according to Schaffer should include such factors as management's motivation for making the change; an understanding of what will really be needed to complete the process; and an assessment of the existing skill level, required resources and an understanding of the pre-existing experience base. Schaffer concludes that plowing ahead without an appreciation for what can actually be accomplished is naïve.

Search for Actions That Will Trigger a Chain Reaction

Recall from chapter one that organizations sometimes go into decline after a history of success. This means that although performance may unravel, the essence of the success formula is probably still in tact. When an unwitting decision gives rise to a dinosaur, it is crucial to be mindful of those aspects of the organization that still add value. Confronting or expelling the dinosaur... must, therefore, undo the decision and reverse the decline in performance without damaging the company or ripping it asunder. The analogy is akin to performing surgery. You don't just make a sweeping incision to remove a tumor and hope you find it. You make a precision cut to reduce the damage to healthy tissue. The same guideline applies here. Since we are not always certain what actions will work or not work, it is useful to introduce punctuated changes to gauge the impact and to minimize risk. Donald Sull, explains, "Even after a company has come to understand the obstacles it faces, it should resist the impulse to rush forward. Some... gurus exhort managers to change every aspect of their companies simultaneously to foment revolution... The assumption is that old formulas need to be thrown to the wind... But the veterans of change programs... argue against that approach. They say that by trying to change everything all at once, managers often destroy crucial competencies, tear the fabric of social relationships that took years to weave and disorient customers and employees alike. A revolution provides a shock to the system, but the shock sometimes proves to be fatal[13]". As a case in point, Sull describes what happened to Firestone, a once very successful company that responded to its challenge in a way that compromised its future. The introduction of the radial tire actually did not catch the company by surprise. In fact, Firestone reacted promptly. Unfortunately, it reacted in a way that split its focus and created two competing commitments that increased cost and compromised quality. Firestone invested in radial tire production and responded quickly to the threat of a substitute product, but it delayed in closing many plants that produced traditional tires. It failed to break the tie! Once again, we see that the way that managers interpret and enact their environment is of more consequence than are the external factors. According to Sull, "by 1979 the company was in deep trouble". In 1980, the board hired an outside CEO to turnaround Firestone. He closed plants, canceled longstanding customer relationships, modified the capital process and replaced many key executives with outside talent. Allegedly, "the team of outside managers disposed of several of Firestones most promising businesses and invested heavily in tire retailing, despite warnings from seasoned insiders that the company's tire stores never had been profitable. Although the company was saved, Firestone never recuperated. It was bought by Bridgestone and experienced yet another setback with the recall of millions of tires and a battle with Ford, one of its largest and oldest customers.

To avoid such outcomes, a punctuated approach searches for actions that will trigger a chain reaction. Such actions or catalytic mechanisms[14], as Jim Collins likes to call them, target changes in policies or work practices that produce a ripple effect. It is not always known or understood how the action will impact an organization. As such, the action needs to be metered and relatively low risk. The intent is to poke and probe until the management team gets a fix on how to expel the dinosaur from its living room. Once the change produces a desired outcome, subsequent actions follow to expand the scope and financial impact. Consider the following example:

A tier one automotive supplier struggled to regain its former success after years of declining performance. Rather than attempt a large-scale transformation, management decided to target one facet of the company, and to use it as a platform to catalyze further change. Since material expense accounted for over two thirds of the cost of sales and the complaints about suppliers were abundant, it seemed like a good place to start. There was no awareness of dinosaurs or competing strategies at this early stage. To get started, a team conducted an in-depth review of purchasing and supplier management practices. They soon learned that purchasing did not participate in the quote development or cost estimating processes. Instead, they were relegated to administering purchase orders, expediting parts and tracking open issues. They found that almost any department could make sourcing decisions independent of purchasing. For example, program managers had the authority to change suppliers in the middle of a program or once a program launched, regardless of the switching costs. Discussions with suppliers revealed that a single supplier might receive conflicting instructions from a half dozen different persons for the same project. They discovered that there were no pre-qualified suppliers, even though 85% of total material costs were commodities. Without any pre-qualified suppliers, it became nearly impossible to factor process capabilities into the equation which meant that it was difficult to produce good product specifications. Without good product specs, suppliers frequently produced bad parts. In addition, suppliers were often released to make parts before acceptance criteria were finalized, thus, causing false starts, scrap and excessive rework. To compensate for the ongoing rework, suppliers generally increased their price to cover the added cost. Such practices contributed to a constant rotation of suppliers. This cycle repeated itself over and over despite awareness that the practices needed change. People we talked with knew that such practices escalated warranty costs; eroded the overall profitability of the product over its life cycle; incurred staggering switching costs; and caused poor quality. Still the practices continued and succumbed to pressure to meet short-term demands and deadlines.

Because these practices were informal and tangled, undoing the myriad activities and changing years of avoidance behavior would be difficult. Moreover, it was hard to know whether changing any of the practices would be harmful. Rather than change every longstanding practice and run the risk of disrupting the company or starting a political battle, the team limited its focus to just two key policy changes. First, they enacted a policy that made any decision to switch or to de-source a supplier a corporate decision. This meant that no one could take unilateral action without first going before the senior management team. Second, the team issued a policy to all suppliers that purchasing was the only voice that could authorize suppliers to act, expend dollars or change specifications. Since purchasing issued purchase orders and controlled supplier invoices, the suppliers complied. The two changes had profound impact. For example, by making the decision to switch a supplier the sole domain of corporate, the constant turnover of suppliers stopped. The supply base stabilized; and suppliers that made the cut became pre-qualified strategic partners. Once a group of pre-qualified suppliers was established, the purchasing function assigned primary accountability to the commodity buyers to work more closely with them. Since there were few buyers with commodity experience and the skills needed to assess a supplier's ability, new ones were added. The new buyers were now capable of conducting supplier reviews. The buyers worked closely with the supply base and gained a better understanding of their capabilities and technology. As such, the suppliers began to participate in quote development and provided a broader range of technical solutions than ever before. These improvements shortened the overall lead-time and reduced costs and rework.

The decision to make purchasing the only voice to authorize a supplier to act caused others in the company to modify their behavior. For example, unless a risk assessment existed, purchasing would not release a supplier to expend money. This forced the program team to clearly define product and part specification and acceptance criteria and prompted engineering to adopt standard design guidelines. Otherwise, purchasing refused to release a supplier to move forward. This chain reaction trued up the system, stopped costly shortcuts and practices, reduced warranty and material costs and thrust the company into a new era of professional supply chain management.

The example shows that a few well-placed punctuated interventions can make a significant difference without plunging the organization into an all-out bureaucratic, labor-intensive change process. The intent is to minimize disruption to the organization while introducing incremental improvements. However, the changes should not be isolated or disconnected. Instead, they should be designed to make additional changes obvious. In large part, selecting an intervention depends on how managers frame the challenge. Based on the work that Gilbert and Bowers did at Harvard, they found that "management practices that create a crisis exploit the human tendency to respond with greater energy and commitment when we feel threatened than when we feel safe[15]". They also found, however, that "when the motivation to change comes from feeling threatened, managers and teams usually respond not just aggressively, but rigidly: They focus on defending the existing business model (as opposed to creating a new one); they commit resources in large lump sums (rather than in staged investments); and they tighten the existing organization authority (instead of giving... autonomy)[16]". The last thing that managers need to expel a dinosaur is more rigidity. It is for such reasons that the managerial response be framed as an opportunity as opposed to a threat. A comprehensive change will almost always be seen as a threat by at least a few stakeholders, because it seeks to change longstanding practices and power bases. In contrast, inserting a few policies that are tailored to the change being contemplated tends to mollify anxieties or defensiveness, and to increase the chances that the intervention will trigger a positive chain reaction.

Find More than One Way to Win

Since it is not always clear what actions will reverse a decline in performance caused by a dinosaur, it is useful to employ a multifaceted approach. This means that managers need to find more than one way to attack the dinosaur. Too many managers jump to single solutions or to ones that may have worked in the past. As a result, they limit the chances of success by creating all or nothing scenarios. For example, I worked with the director of an insurance company who was given the assignment to reduce the cost of long-term disability products. During the work session with him, he locked onto revising the existing software program to flag key data and to signal the administrators to properly code charges and, thus, avoid incurring unnecessary costs. Despite my urging to consider other options, he remained locked onto the one solution. It dawned on me to ask him what happens if this action does not work. He stared at me blankly and said, "What do you mean?" I again asked if the single solution did not achieve the cost target, what he would do. Only then did he realize that one action might not hit the goal or worse yet, would cause him to start over, thereby, missing his deadline.

Confronted by the need to improve profit, managers will install a new ERP system and spend millions of dollars in hopes that a single solution will improve performance. Thus far, there is little data that shows a return on investment for ERP systems. The trap is that managers do not have the desired outcome clearly defined. Instead, the implementation of the tasks and activities become the focus – not the end result. When the single solution fails or falls short of expectations (as it many times does) to produce the intended result, the change process must start from scratch again. Starting over causes interest to wane and reinforces the belief that trying to change is a waste of time. Losing faith early in a change process is definitely not desirable for rooting out a dinosaur from a system. To avoid this possibility, managers can focus on a tangible result or outcome to start, rather than become preoccupied with an activity. Getting the end in mind first, opens the range of options, whereas focusing on solutions runs the risk of rework and repetition. Consider the following case[17].

The Dinosaur in the Living Room

The staff of a residential mental health facility suffered injuries and high worker compensation costs while lifting and transferring patients. A quick review showed that as the patient population changed, the required number of lifts and transfers also increased. However, the equipment needed was not available. The solution seemed obvious – order the equipment needed to perform lifts and transfers. Even after the equipment arrived and was in use, injuries continued at the same rate. To reconcile the problem, management decided to set a goal this time to reduce the number of safety incidents related to lifts and transfers by fifty percent within two months. This subtle, yet key shift from solutions to end results prompted the staff to explore *more than one way to win*. In addition to using the newly ordered equipment, the staff considered safer methods for lifting and transferring patients. They also discovered that two patients in particular accounted for almost half of the injuries and that such incidents occurred almost always during a change in shifts (something they already knew). The staff decided to handle these two patients differently and limited lifts and transfers to times when more staff was available. Scheduling changes were also made to bolster staffing during crunch periods in the morning and evening. Once implemented, the variety of actions reduced the incidents per month from 42 to19 in a matter of two months, a 57% drop.

By focusing energy on a specific result, the staff freed themselves to consider a broader array of options that would reduce injuries. It was clear that simply adding new equipment did nothing to stop injuries. Moreover, targeting a specific outcome enabled the staff to access solutions that were obvious and that drew from a variety of different staff – not just purchasing. One of Steven Covey's seven habits of highly successful people urges that we "begin with the end in mind[18]". Covey explains, "It is incredibly easy to get caught up in an activity trap, in the busyness of life, to work harder and harder at climbing the ladder... only to discover it's leaning against the wrong wall. It is possible to be busy – very busy – without being very effective". In the case of the mental health facility, that is exactly what happened. The staff busied themselves with the purchase of new equipment under the mistaken assumption that a single solution would stop injuries. Buying new equipment supplanted the real goal - reducing or eliminating injuries and decreasing workers compensation costs. Jumping to single solutions or focusing on activities to the exclusion of end results is a higher risk and lower probability strategy. Only by increasing the number of ways to win did the staff reduce injuries.

Make Effective Tradeoffs...

As the Rolling Stone's song refrains, "You can't always get what you want to..." Trying to overcome avoidance behaviors and tackle the obvious is tricky business. It is tricky because the behaviors are defensive and self protective. For example, the plant manager described in Chapter Two did not want to add staff to the furnace forming room because he felt he would lose face with the employees and the union. The only way he would increase staffing levels was by assigning the employees to temporary, rather than permanent status. This small (yet transparent) tradeoff mitigated his anxiety and allowed him enough of a buffer zone to confront the dinosaur and to take obvious action. Tradeoffs may appear insignificant or even wimpy, but such actions create momentum and provide air cover for the key actors in the system. Changes can be viewed as having a half-life; and as such, managers should search for ways of cutting the distance between the current and desired state in half, even if it takes multiple iterations. One approach for cutting the distance in half is to look for meaningful nuances and to differentiate the challenge. To illustrate:

The president of a design and concept development firm balked at the thought of trimming staff in the face of declining profits. She had just finished a banner year that earned her accolades for achieving an eight million dollar turnaround. The reversal of fortune was due to an explicit strategy to evolve into customer specific business units, and to adopt a strong customer intimate approach. This meant that they dedicated entire facilities and staff to their major customers and located their operations in close geographic proximity to them. They funded projects ahead of the growth curve and sometimes in advance of approvals. They participated on key committees and customized responses according to their customer's needs and priorities. They even expanded services beyond what they might normally have offered to other less strategic customers. As the strategy and business model unfolded, however, they retained a commitment to the headquarters that once housed all of the staff and activities. The headquarters operation soon became redundant and costly in comparison to the success of the satellite offices and dedicated customer sites. When the economy tanked and customers demanded large price concessions, they found themselves faced with mounting losses and little time to react. At first, the president reluctantly concluded that she could no longer support the existing structure. If she shifted to the satellite model and abandoned headquarters, she could reduce the breakeven point by two million dollars, survive the downtown and compete for bids more effectively. Although she knew what needed to be done, she got cold feet and began to back peddle. Rather than insist that the president implement the desired change, the CEO asked the president to convert the headquarters into another customer dedicated satellite office that the president immediately embraced. However, the CEO also imposed a time limit and demanded that a contingency plan be drafted in the event that revenues and profits failed to materialize. Although the president still did not want to break the tie between two competing business models, the tradeoff allowed her time to adjust, consider the alternative and to take action that was modest and less anxiety producing.

Psychologists have long understood that reinforcing the right behavior or discouraging the wrong behavior oftentimes must be done in steps. Shaping behavior gradually tends to work because the criteria at the outset are less rigorous[19]. Over time, however, the standards increase and become more demanding. By setting iterative standards and expectations, managers adjust gradually and warm up to the changes they know are warranted. The idea, here, is to find tradeoffs that are approximations of the end results, but, nonetheless, move the ball incrementally toward the goal line. There is no need to coerce, convince or contrive. Instead, managers adopt a bargaining stance and ask the question, "If you are not willing to do (fill in the blank), what are you willing to do." This tack forces key players and potential blockers to respond in kind. They must take a modest step forward with the understanding that it is only one of a series of punctuated steps. And for those of you, who are impatient, remember that you can actually go farther faster using an incremental approach, than by going for all the marbles at once.

Summary

Using punctuated and incremental strategies represents an important means of expelling a dinosaur from the living room. The purpose of this step is to generate momentum and to mobilize action. Using punctuated strategies takes the nature of human behavior into account and acknowledges that managers may be risk averse or can become anxious, when faced with difficult or embarrassing challenges. Unfortunately, traditional responses to change often ignore such considerations and are, therefore, less effective options for dislodging a dinosaur from the living room or tackling the obvious. Rather than succumb to such mistakes and ignore the obvious, this chapter poses several alternatives that subscribe to punctuated strategies. These incremental approaches have several advantages. To start, a punctuated strategy keeps the change effort manageable and limited in scope. This action also increases the chances of success; allows people to make mistakes and to develop skills and capabilities at a reasonable pace. Second, an incremental approach keeps anxiety at a lower level so as not to overwhelm the organization and its key players. *Building the capability of the organization by terracing improvement efforts; working with existing limitations; searching for actions that will trigger a chain reaction; finding more than one way to win; and making effective tradeoffs...* are five alternatives for generating momentum without the negative by-products that are often linked to the misaligned responses described in chapter two. For example, *building the capability of the organization by terracing improvement efforts* acknowledges that everyone does not always have the skills needed to affect the types of change needed to reverse a decline in performance. *Working with inherent limitations* imposes common sense by recognizing that you cannot always eat steak and that sometimes hamburger must do until you can afford better. *Searching for actions that trigger chain reactions* embraces the premise that we do not always know what will work until we take action. Still, it is incumbent on us to experiment on a limited scale to determine, if we can spark a series of positive changes. *Finding more than one way to win* hedges our bet and prevents us from searching for the silver bullet or one best solution. *Making effective tradeoffs* accepts that avoidance and defensiveness are natural, but should not be a reason for letting people off the hook for results. Each of these tactics refuses to accept inherent limitations as an excuse for not making progress or taking action. Instead they insist that punctuated progress is, indeed, possible and can be managed effectively.

Chapter Six

Expel the Dinosaur from the Living Room: Reversing Flawed Decisions and Exiting Negative Spirals

When Robert Bakker asserted that large horned dinosaurs and giant predators were quite capable of galloping at high speeds, he came under immediate attack. According to Bakker, "When I began to publish reconstructions of galloping dinosaurs, the shrill voice of outraged orthodoxy rose to deafening heights[1]". Undaunted by the criticisms, Bakker presented evidence showing that the skeletal structure (e.g., the cnemial crest above the knee and the angle of the shoulder joints) of species such as Triceratops and Tyrannosaurus would, indeed, support speeds that ranged upwards of thirty plus miles per hour. He compared these types of dinosaurs to living mammals such as the rhino (that could reach speeds of thirty-five miles an hour) and again found similar bone structure and support for his assertions. Although there were clearly dinosaurs like Brontosaurus and Stegosaurus that were, indeed, slow, there were many other "multi-ton creatures that could break into a fast-paced charge or get-a-way whenever necessary[2]". Such realizations gained credibility over time such that we accept the possibility today; but it wasn't always the prevailing orthodoxy.

Like Bakker, a management team must remain undaunted and cannot be deterred from taking the right action despite protests to the contrary, once the dinosaur... is known to exist and must be expelled. There will be protests and back tracking, but the management team must stay the course. As explained in prior chapters, management should cultivate an awareness of those sources that foster a dinosaur... so as to avert the pitfalls and traps described in chapter three. It is not always possible to avert such mistakes, however. In those instances, managers need to take accountability and to confront the dinosaur and expose it for what it is (as described in chapter four), rather than act defensively and to pretend that the creature really does not reside in the organization. Once we can talk about a dinosaur in the living room openly, we need to remove it from the organization. Toward this end, a management team can use a punctuated approach (as explained in chapter five) to promote incremental progress, allay anxieties and to minimize risk.

One more set of actions is required to complete the job of expelling the dinosaur. These include: 1) reversing a flawed decision and exiting a negative spiral; 2) maintaining a one-to-one relationship between actions taken and results achieved; and, 3) gaining an in-depth understanding of what caused performance to decline; and what prevented the organization from reversing course, breaking the tie or avoiding obvious improvement opportunities.

Reverse the Flawed Decision and Exit the Negative Spiral...

Reversing a flawed decision or exiting a negative spiral used, here, means that if an organization departs from the original success formula, the management team must undo the decision – not just the decline in performance. If a company grows in non-strategic ways, it must stop doing so and come hard about. If an organization goes outside of its core competencies to fill capacity, it must reverse course and make better use of its capabilities. If a corporation clutters and complicates the landscape with unprofitable products and/or customers, it must jettison such products and customers, contract and adjust, accordingly. If a management team allows individual interest to eclipse organization welfare, it must halt such behavior, replace the offenders and reset the priorities. In each instance, the management team must reverse the negative cycle. It is not

The Dinosaur in the Living Room

enough to improve results. Otherwise, the change will be short lived. Reversing a decision and negative spiral is like untangling a ball of yarn. Dinosaurs do not exist in isolation. They are social in nature. As such, dinosaurs breed more changes and add new variables to the mix that form an integrated, albeit, flawed whole that drives the organization into a negative spiral. This "system of problems,"[3] (or as Akoff prefers to call it - "a mess") derives from the root causes and sources of a dinosaur as described in chapter three. Because the dinosaurs evolve into systems that consist of multiple variables and linkages, action must have direction and purpose. The way out is to focus on reversing the decision. This is exactly what Bain Capital did with the Wesley Jensen Corporation. Rather than live with a $100 million plant geared and tooled to produce standard contact lens, Bain reversed the decision and refocused energies on niche products, even though it required more investment. The electronic manufacturer described in chapter one did the same. Rather than support the existing customer base, management reversed the decision, exited a large number of customers, focused on its core accounts and shrunk the company without wasting any time. Consider the following case:

A contract research organization (CRO) that performed drug testing and scale-up services for the pharmaceutical industry teetered on the brink of losing money each year for five straight years. The primary reason for such dubious results could be traced to the performance of the chemistry group. Although the group was headed by a brilliant scientist and was comprised of a seasoned core of PhD's, they continually experienced cost overruns, on-time completion problems and even exceeded budgeted contingencies. Closer review showed that the contracts that the chemistry group sought tended to involve *de novo* chemistry and, as such, had a much higher degree of uncertainty. According to the scientists, these types of projects just were not predictable. Even when an experiment worked in the lab, there was no guarantee that the drug could be scaled up in the pilot plant to simulate the conditions of mass production. To accommodate these complex projects and the tight deadlines, the chemistry group hired higher caliber staff with advanced degrees and significant industry experience, thus, commanding premium salaries. Such jobs were very attractive to chemists with advanced degrees because the projects provided continued intellectual stimulation. The paradox was that ample opportunities existed to perform very profitable "turn the crank" chemistry projects. However, these types of projects were not very appealing to the chemists with advanced degrees. They explained that "turn the crank" chemistry was better suited to people with bachelors or masters degrees. Unfortunately, management ignored the obvious and continued along the same path until the company was eventually acquired to avoid bankruptcy.

Are you getting the picture? Sometimes organizations unwittingly get caught in what Weick calls a *deviation-amplifying loop*[4]. This is a fancy term for how a series of negative changes (i.e., deviations) link and connect, take root, interact and reinforce one another in ways that create a downward spiral. This system of errors conspires to undo the organization and makes it hard to tell just where or when the problem originated. Weick explains, "A small deviation that is highly probable – such as a wagon breaking down – may develop into a deviation that is very improbable – a city... With sufficient cycling, small deviations can be amplified into complex... events..."[5]. And such amplifying loops can either be negative or positive. In the example described above, this is exactly what happened to the chemistry group and ultimately the contract research organization. They got caught in a downward spiral and reinforcing loop. Management targeted more complex projects (most likely) because they were intellectually challenging; not because the projects would be more profitable. Otherwise, they would have decreased the number of staff with advanced degrees; hired more people with bachelors and masters degrees; and increased the number of more profitable "turn the crank" chemistry projects. They did not even consider this alternative. Instead, they accommodated the situation by adding big name people with advanced degrees at very high salaries. Once on board, however, management felt obligated to retain these high profile scientists, maintain the facade and keep them happy by seeking more *de novo* chemistry projects. In essence, they were more afraid of losing the scientists than earning a profit.

Maintain a One-to-One Relationship between Actions Taken and Results Achieved

Maintaining a one to one relationship between actions taken and results achieved is another important aspect of purging a dinosaur from one's living room. It ensures that there is no wasted motion. Every action must count. Every arrow must have a target to hit. There should be no studies or lengthy data collection efforts. There are no outside programs, systems or fads introduced. There is no "smart talk[6]" that serves as a proxy for action. Instead, every action is simple, straightforward and designed to reverse declining performance or to produce results. It is easy to say and very hard to do. Many years ago Robert Schaffer wrote, "...instead of focusing directly on achieving measurable end results (like lower costs, better quality and faster turnaround time), many... never get beyond the preparatory stage. The assumption is that once there has been enough gearing up, enough training and enough investment, results will someday emerge like Venus rising from the sea"[7]. To avoid such scenarios, managers must ask whether the actions they plan to take will, indeed, make a difference in the situation. I am not asking managers to use a crystal ball and to predict the future. Instead, I'm asking managers to apply an acid test. If managers find themselves planning, doing more data collection, conducting more analyses or performing other preparatory activities, then the actions will not lead to results. Actions of this nature are considered foreplay. This insistence may frustrate some managers because they've been conditioned to do so or are frustrated scientists. It simply does not apply in this case, since dinosaurs and obvious challenges are sustained through avoidance and inaction – not testing. To reinforce the relationship between action and results, it is easier if the actions are abbreviated and short term in nature (i.e., 100 days or less), rather than elongated. Doing so forces people to narrow the scope of the effort into a sharp, yet manageable task, and limits the temptation to search for outside solutions or to defer to lengthy programs, systems or fads. Once a hundred day plan is set, do not accept excuses or explanations that nothing can be done in such a time frame. It can. Nonetheless, if the result truly cannot be achieved in less than 100 days, then the effort or project can be broken into sub-goals and/or sub-teams so it can. Do not compromise.

 Let's revisit the Wesley Jensen case described above. Wesley Jensen, a specialty contact lens maker, formerly owned by Shering Plough, made colored and "toric" contact lens that were used to correct astigmatism. In the early 1990's the company, hoping to grow, entered into the larger standard contact lens market, a departure from its original success formula and business model. By entering the standard contact lens market, Wesley Jensen found itself competing with the likes of Johnson & Johnson and Bausch & Lomb, two formidable rivals. By 1995, the company was losing money and in a perilous cash position[8] because it lacked the economies of scale that its larger competitors enjoyed. When Bain Capital, a private equity firm, bought Wesley Jensen, the new management team decided the company needed to return to its core specialty contact lens business. A series of quick and focused actions ensued. "A new $100 million factory (built to produce standard lenses) was quickly retooled to make specialty lenses. The company stopped serving unprofitable customers such as high volume retail optometry chains. It cut spending on advertising, promotions and other outside services and eliminated many positions, including several layers of management in manufacturing. At the same time, it expanded its product range within the specialty segment and made selective acquisitions to bolster its leadership position in the core market"[9]. Operating profit jumped to 15% and when a public offering was rendered in 1997 a forty-five fold return on equity was achieved in less than two years.

Recall the opening case from chapter one. Once the management team discovered that a large portion of its customer base was not profitable, it moved rapidly to reconcile the situation. The management team jettisoned several hundred of their unprofitable customers through price increases, diversion to distributors and other exit strategies. Concurrent with the customer consolidation effort, the management team combined three plants into one facility, sold off inventory and finished goods, and refocused energies on making core products. In addition, they reduced indirect expense by reducing headcount. Last, renewed sales efforts refocused energy on the top 50-60 customers in order to recoup the loss in sales due to the initial customer consolidation. Net operating profits tripled. Return on net assets doubled. And all of the sales that were lost due to pruning the customer base were recouped from new sales. The entire set of activities took no more than nine months to fully enact.

The two examples show that once a management team knows they have a dinosaur in the living room; confronts what they have been ignoring; and gauges the level of risk and anxiety the company can reasonably absorb; a series of sharply focused, short burst activities launch to improve performance and to rekindle organizational spirit. Every action taken produced results and reversed the decline in performance.

In studying two thousand private equity transactions over the past ten years, Rogers, Holland and Haas found that groups like Texas Pacific Group, Berkshire Partners, Bain Capital, Perima and EQT delivered annual returns greater than 50% year after year and fund after fund[10]. They explained that private equity (PE) firms focus all their energies on accelerating the growth of the value of their business through the relentless pursuit of just one or two key initiatives. They narrow their sights to widen their profits[11]". The key difference is that PE firms approach the challenge with a short time frame because they know they will sell the acquisition in 3-5 years. As such, there is no time to waste. In fact, many PE firms create a 100-day plan that is based on an investment thesis (a clear statement of how they will make the business more valuable…). And the investment thesis directs all actions, accordingly. For example, when Bain Capital acquired Wesley Jensen (described above) the investment thesis was, "Return the company to its core business". Immediately upon closing the deal, the 100-day plan started. Such models provide managers with a roadmap for ensuring that there is a one to one relationship between actions taken and results achieved.

Ensure That Actions Foster Learning...

Ensuring that actions produce learning in addition to results is another key component of reversing the decision and exiting a negative spiral. But what types of action foster learning; and what types of learning are we trying to produce? There are two types of learning we want to achieve and there are several types of actions that lead to such learning. The two types of learning are corrective and transformative. *Corrective learning* stems from solving problems, applying past knowledge and experience to the current situation, finding simple cause and effect relationships and detecting and correcting mistakes. Argyris calls this type of learning "single loop learning"[12] because there is a straightforward link between actions and results. You can see the impact and draw the linkage. He explains, "Learning occurs when an organization achieves what is intended; that is, there is a match between its *design for action* and the actuality or outcome. Learning also occurs when a mismatch between intention and outcome is identified and corrected; that is, a mismatch is turned into a match... Whenever an error is detected and corrected *without questioning or altering the underlying values* of the system... the learning is single loop"[13]. Confronting and expelling a dinosaur from the living room requires corrective action, and thus learning. Moreover, corrective or single loop learning is vital to day-to-day functioning. Organizations that do not engage in corrective learning, once errors are discovered, face larger scale and more radical changes on down the road.

Toward this end, reversing a decision and exiting a negative spiral are effective means for preventing dinosaurs from resurfacing.

Transformative learning is different. *Transformative learning* comes from directly challenging the steering mechanisms that guide the organization, provide consistency and govern its members' behavior. "Steering mechanisms are implied messages, values, practices, assumptions, unstated rules and expected behaviors[14]" that evolve over time in response to the environment and to top management preferences. Although it is hard to touch or feel such mechanisms, they, nonetheless, shape choices and direct behavior at all levels of the company. Such mechanisms have little to do with explicitly improving performance metrics (e.g., reducing inventory, cutting scrap, increasing efficiency, etc.). They have everything to do with understanding why members of the organization are unable or unwilling to act on clear performance improvement opportunities; or to explain why a team acts defensively, when asked why they ignored/avoided the obvious for months or even years. Many people learn that if they act consistently with the steering mechanisms, they remain safe, can avoid conflict, painful situations or assaults on their ego. Adhering to the organization's steering mechanisms is one reason why managers delay and are reluctant to respond even when a decline in performance unfolds. Tackling these types of practices involve harder, more complex questions and choices. Nonetheless, understanding steering mechanisms are quite pivotal because steering mechanisms hold a dinosaur in place long after it is discovered. For example, when asked why a management team was unwilling to exit unprofitable products and customers, the VP of Sales responded, "We don't fire our customers". Many managers shy away from tough questions like, "Why don't we fire our customers" or "Under what circumstances would we fire our customers," because it will presumably create conflict. Unless action is taken to get at the reasoning process and to open a window into the underlying thoughts, the actions will be limited to corrective ones which may be necessary, but not sufficient to effect a complete change. Let's examine in more detail what types of actions yield the two types of learning.

Actions that Foster Corrective Learning

Actions that produce corrective learning involve the mechanics of improving performance. Such actions might include making concrete adjustments to a work process; targeting root causes of poor performance; or introducing new elements or skills needed to bridge the gap between current and future states. These activities are the nuts and bolts of reversing a decline in performance and getting rid of the dinosaur in the living room. For example, recall the company that added a second production line at great expense. Faced with higher fixed cost, the management team moved quickly to fill the new line with unrelated and lower volume products. They soon learned that the decision to run new products with which they were unfamiliar caused profits, productivity and quality to decline. Indeed, there was a mismatch between intent and actual outcomes. Once the source of the dinosaur (i.e., moving outside of core competencies to fill capacity) was discovered, several expedient actions were taken to correct the mistake. Core products were reassigned and scheduled on the original production line, even though it did not fill it completely. This action immediately improved productivity and labor efficiency, reduced scrap and boosted profitability. This was the first set of corrective actions and learning for those involved. They could see first hand how changing the mechanics of the situation produced improvement – a key lesson they already knew, but had to relearn. Next, since the company could not exit the new products immediately without triggering a lawsuit or bad press, the decision was made to organize a focused factory around the new asset. This isolated the unrelated products until the time was right to exit them. By isolating the problem from the mainstream products, the crew working on the new line also discovered that they could recycle scrapped material and further minimize losses. As shown, each action involved solving a problem and applying past experience and knowledge to the existing situation; and each action produced corrective learning and insights that could be incorporated into people's memory for future reference.

Actions that Foster Transformative Learning

Actions designed to foster *transformative learning* do not stop after corrections are made. Transformative actions seek to understand why people were unable or unwilling to make changes that were obvious or already known. This type of learning seeks answers to the origin of the dinosaur, how it came about and sustained itself over time. Applying this type of inquiry to the example cited above required the management team to explain why they added a new production line. Asking such a question almost immediately elicits defensiveness. The intent, here is not to engender defensiveness. Defensiveness is the last thing we want. Instead, the purpose is to foster honesty and candid discussion including the admission of mistakes without the fear of reprisal and what can be learned from them. This type of discussion should be akin to a peer review that doctors and other professionals engage in to teach interns and younger practitioners. It is okay if such discussion is aggressive so long as everyone knows the purpose is to learn from the experience. It is vital to understand what led up to the decision and the reasoning behind it. In this instance, the management team was perfectly happy to let sleeping dogs lie; especially when profits returned to normal and the business was on track again. Ignoring what happened would compound the avoidance behavior. To generate maximum learning, we pushed the team to review what happened and to gain insight into the process. It turned out that one of the "steering mechanisms[15]" was a rule designed to promote growth. Once a division hit a certain level of sales, management was to either spin off a new division or business or to expand capacity. However, interpreting the rule literally without a strategy or new customers to support the expansion; or a game plan for how they would fill the added capacity, was never intended. Some members of the management team recalled that they questioned the accuracy of the sales forecast and admitted that they felt adding another line was a mistake. In the very first discussions with the team, several managers said that they knew exactly when their problems began. However, they failed to voice their concerns at the time other than in private conversations. When sales did not materialize, the management team panicked and acted to absorb the fixed expense with unrelated products. They did not want upper management to get involved in their daily affairs – another example of defensive reasoning. The paradox was that the sharp decline in performance had the exact opposite effect. Senior management's attention was instantly attracted. Rather than admit the extra production line was a mistake, they tried to fill its capacity with cats and dogs.

Even after we discover the dinosaur in the living room, the job does not stop. The actions that managers take must continue to prompt deeper learning that comes from more than conceptual work or correcting mistakes and flaws. The assumption is that when managers discover inconsistencies between the desired outcomes and what actually occurs, they will reconcile such gaps. We now know that this is not the case. Otherwise, dinosaurs could not exist. In studies conducted by Argyris and Schon[16], they found that "... only when persons could alter their actions without examining their governing variables (e.g., listen more or ask specific questions)" would they correct mistakes. However, "if the error produced mistrust, rather than trust, correcting it was not simple... Before they are willing to take such action, they must examine their fears about what others may do to them...[17]" I believe Deming had it right, when he said that an organization must extract fear from its midst, if it is to achieve higher levels of performance.

Summary

Reversing a decision and exiting a negative spiral seek to finish the job of expelling a dinosaur from the living room. The tendency is to underestimate what will be needed to reconcile a decline in performance or to take advantage of an immediate opportunity. Above all else, action is needed to generate tangible results, insights and learning. Without highly directed action there can be no grounded learning – only speculation based on lack of testing. Achieving the desired outcome, thus, requires that a management team reverses the fundamental decision that fostered a decline in performance or that acted as a ceiling on the organization's potential. It also requires the management team to extricate itself from the course of action in which it is embedded, if it is flawed. Single variable changes designed to reduce discomfort will not fully work. The fundamental and resulting negative spiral and mess have to be untangled and the direction reversed. This can be achieved by maintaining a one to one ratio of actions taken to results achieved, since doing so prevents avoidance or stalling. Last, the full cycle of action is considered complete, once the management team takes the time to reflect and to candidly identify those behaviors, injunctions, long standing practices or steering mechanisms that prevented the team from confronting the dinosaur or acting on an obvious opportunity. Reflection of this type fosters two forms of learning – corrective and transformative. Whereas, corrective learning is key to the mechanics of improving performance, transformative learning is crucial to understanding the underlying behaviors that block progress. Insights derived from this kind of reflection explain why the team interpreted and enacted the situation the way it did.

All organizations make mistakes. It is simply part of an organization's search for variety and growth. Some mistakes turn into successes and other experiments simply remain mistakes. The difference is not whether the management team discovers the mistakes, but whether they do something about it quickly, once they discover it was, indeed, a mistake. In Built to Last[18], the authors found that the best in class companies "tried a lot of stuff", made a lot of mistakes, kept those that worked and discarded those that did not. The difference between the best companies and the rest was the degree to which the management teams were able to "branch" into new endeavors while "pruning" those moves that did not pan out. Regardless of the outcome, organizations that develop the mindset, capacity & skills to recover from mistakes will remain unafraid to test new ideas. They can acknowledge the errors and remedy the situation in short order, while capturing vital learning for future reference.

Chapter Seven

Challenging Conventional Wisdom: The Managerial Heresies

Many years ago I read a book called <u>The Dinosaur Heresies</u> by Robert Bakker. If you could not tell, it had a profound impact on my thinking; and not because the topic was about dinosaurs. At the time it was published there were myriad theories and pre-conceived notions about dinosaurs. Some theories asserted that dinosaurs were cold blooded. Others assumed they were lizard-like with splayed legs. Some suggested that dinosaurs evolved continuously. Still other theories suggested the dinosaurs were lumbering creatures and could not move rapidly. Bakker systematically debunked theory after theory using a base of long forgotten knowledge, straightforward logic and down to earth reasoning. In particular, Bakker's heresies were rooted in data drawn from studies conducted decades earlier. When these theories were originally introduced, they were ignored or placed on a shelf to collect dust because they ran counter to prevailing orthodoxy. Undaunted, Bakker dusted off the old studies to corroborate his own findings and produced a new set of assertions and practical implications for the field of paleontology.

Perhaps the parallels between paleontology and management are a stretch. However, I think there are some good lessons to learn. Most certainly, there is some practical advice for managing change in addition to averting, confronting and expelling a dinosaur from the living room. These arguments stem from the suggested tactics and practices presented in the preceding chapters. Specifically, there are four implications that might be applied as general rules of thumb.

Worry More About Correcting Mistakes Than Making Them...

We can now see that managers and entire organizations can experience a decline in performance despite their best intentions. Like the paleontologists, however, they tend to ignore, avoid or act contrary to their instincts or to data that is readily available to them. This should be no surprise to anyone. Avoidance is a well-founded characteristic of human behavior and sometimes a very functional defense mechanism. Therefore, avoiding mistakes cannot always be the primary preoccupation. Managers and leaders unwittingly make mistakes (as described in chapter three) oftentimes under the banner of growth. Since the sources of a dinosaur in the living room and the resulting decline in performance cannot always be averted, the focus should shift toward developing the capacity and resilience to recover quickly and completely from such occurrences. Developing such resilience requires, as a first step, the ability to confront reality as it is. Diane Coutu, a senior editor of Harvard Business Review explains that resilience, in large part, stems from facing reality in a forthright manner and asking, "Do I truly understand – and accept – the reality of my situation? Does my organization? Those are good questions because... research suggests most people slip into denial as a coping mechanism.[1]" To ensure that we "truly understand and accept" our situation, and are prepared for the inevitability of making errors, it is incumbent on us to: 1) align our responses to the forces that are driving the demand for better performance; 2) ground those responses in the realization that there is less time to do more work with fewer resources than ever before (as presented in chapter two); 3) identify and understand the sources from which dinosaurs emerge so a management team can avert such pitfalls (as explained in chapter three); and 4) confront and expel a dinosaur, if it does rear its head, by making it possible to talk openly; and finding ways to make new choices by reducing the level of anxiety by using punctuated strategies and reversing flawed decisions and/or exiting negative spirals (as described in chapters four through six).

Use a Different Mindset & Challenge Conventional Wisdom

Managers need to do more than just detect and correct mistakes. They need to understand the behaviors that prevent an organization from confronting the dinosaur when it first appears; or that preclude managers from acting on obvious opportunities that will improve performance. Such reflection and action require a very different mindset – one that departs from conventional wisdom and prevailing managerial thought. To evoke a different mindset, I offered a series of implied *managerial heresies* throughout this book that fly in the face of conventional wisdom and prevailing managerial thought. These heresies seek to replace, heretofore, accepted change practices (see Table 7.1) with ones that are more in tune with what works and the realities in which organizations now find themselves. There are five managerial heresies to consider, when responding to the need for better performance:

Harlow B. Cohen

Table 7.1: Replace Conventional Wisdom with Managerial Heresies...

Conventional Wisdom	Managerial Heresies
Huge gains in performance are not possible...	Huge gains in performance are possible using existing resources in relatively short time frames...
Environmental factors have more consequence on performance than does the way in which a management team interprets and enacts such factors...	The way that a management team interprets and enacts its environment has more consequence on performance than does the environmental factors themselves...
Maintaining a constant vigil to change is desirable...	Change is not always desirable...
Total systems change is a necessary prerequisite to achieve gains or to reconcile declines in performance...	Incremental/punctuated change strategies are preferred; total systems change is not always necessary or desirable...
Performance improvement is linked to abstract and/or intermediate variables such as culture, structure, style, etc...	Potential is unleashed when a management team breaks the tie between competing elements...

Heresy #1: Large gains in performance are possible in relatively short time frames by using existing resources. Whereas, some believe that gains of twenty-five, fifty, one hundred percent or more are unrealistic; there are organizations that actually achieved three and four times their bottom line in less than a year and in some instances in a matter of months. Such gains occurred without introducing additional resources. Quite the contrary, the gains came without the advent of additional technology, resources or capital. Once a management team decides to confront the big ugly truth facing their organization, they typically discover one or two very large opportunities. These are the opportunities that hold the potential to achieve huge gains, provided mangers are willing to think differently and to acknowledge the avoidance behaviors and defense mechanisms that hide that potential.

Heresy #2: The way that managers interpret and enact their organization is of more consequence than external or environmental factors. As shown in chapter three, managers do not always read the tea leaves correctly. Instead, managers, at times, enact a form of growth that has the opposite effect because it is strategically or fundamentally flawed or does not fit the circumstances. It is for such reasons that change programs have a low success ratio – because the managers do not understand the context or circumstances in which the organization is embedded before they decide to install an external change program. No one can fault the desire to grow, but we can certainly question the way that a management team brackets its organizational experience, interprets its environment and implements the improvement process. As Christenson & Raynor explain, "Good theories… are circumstance contingent: They define not just what causes what and why, but also how the causal mechanism will produce different outcomes in different situations[2]."

Heresy #3: Change is not always a good thing. Given the growing number of publications that urge managers to maintain a constant vigil to change and to stay abreast of change, it is not surprising that they've become conditioned into thinking that change is always desirable. It's not! There are times that change is not appropriate or warranted. Changing when the market does not require revision can prompt a decline in performance needlessly and prematurely. Adding competing strategies that dilute the focus or that tax the allocation of limited resources, likewise, will cause performance to decline. Again, the question is not whether to change, but when to change, how to change and under what circumstances to change.

Heresy #4: Comprehensive and total systems solutions have high risks and a low probability of achieving the desired outcomes because these approaches overwhelm the organization. Whereas, many think that the only way to achieve dramatic results is by using a total systems approach, we now understand that not only is it not necessary, but that a total systems approach is a high-risk endeavor. Such large-scale efforts tend not to produce the desired outcomes, and are too complex for an organization to absorb while trying to run day-to-day activities. Many studies and data show that these types of change programs have poor track records. In comparison, when management teams replace a total systems mentality with a punctuated approach, they tend to produce better results in less time because progress is achieved in incremental bites; and anxiety is kept at a manageable pitch.

Heresy #5: Breaking the tie between competing elements unleashes huge gains in performance. Many advocates of external change programs believe that performance improvement is linked to such factors as culture, structure, style and the like. Many of these variables are either abstract or intermediate in nature. They are not, however, causal. I used to believe that to produce performance improvement or to reverse a performance shortfall that the culture needed to change first. I came to realize that if I expected culture to change, I would be waiting a very long time. Culture is too abstract for people to get their arms around and it is the last element to change, not the first. Changes in culture are the consequence of people generating results by experimenting with new ways of working. Rather than focus on intermediate or abstract variables, managers can reconcile declining performance or unleash dramatic potential when they focus energies on breaking the tie between competing strategies, business models or beliefs; and when they maintain a one-to-one relationship between actions taken and results achieved. When they do so, they commit to a single, focused course of action and eliminate distraction.

The argument behind each heresy is that we should consider human nature whenever we design change and improvement efforts. This advice is old, but nonetheless, urges us to become more astute observers of not just our own behavior, but the behavior of others. Douglas McGregor recognized the importance of designing work systems that are consistent with human nature decades ago, when he wrote his classic, <u>The Human Side of Enterprise</u>. The paradox is that none of us are a mystery to anyone except, perhaps, ourselves. And if none of us are mysteries, then it means that human nature is obvious. Therefore, ignoring human nature causes us to overlook the obvious, and overlooking the obvious enables dinosaurs in the living room to surface and performance to decline.

Act on the Obvious...

The above ideas build on the obvious and observable, not the dramatic or innovative. When I share such thoughts with managers, they tend to nod in agreement. They seem to already know what I am saying. Yet, they act in contradiction to what they know. Pfeffer & Sutton expressed this realization best when they explained, "We now live in a world where knowledge transfer and information exchange are tremendously efficient, and where there are numerous organizations in the business of collecting and transferring best practices. So, there are fewer and smaller differences in what firms know than in their ability to act on that knowledge"[3]. Hence, the major difference between good and great organizations resides in their ability to mobilize action based on what they already know. It is for such reasons that I am not in the least bit flattered, when I receive confirmation of my assertions. I already know there is a pervasive defensiveness at work; and, it is this defensiveness that causes managers to ignore, avoid, deny or delay acting on what they know they should do. Acting on the obvious and confronting avoidance behaviors are critical because something is very different today than it was even ten years ago. As explained in chapter two, there is less time to do more work with fewer resources than ever before. The combination of downsizing, industry consolidation, mature markets, the compression of cycle times and the emphasis on speed make it a top priority to use interventions that have high payoff, yet are less labor intensive. We, therefore, cannot afford to ignore the obvious or waste precious time. If we do, we'll experience the same questionable track record associated with ineffective change programs that we have for the past three decades. Why? Because we avoided the basics, ignored our instincts and did not bolster the confidence that was needed to go along with our convictions. Too many traditional change methods are either labor intensive, have a low payoff or both. It is for such reasons that confronting the dinosaur in the living room represents an important alternative to consider, especially when an organization goes into decline. And going into decline is not a question of if. It is a question of when.

Don't Just Sit There – Do Something...

Management teams simply need to act on the opportunities that are available to them before the threat of external events steals the initiative; forces them to take the type of action they fear most; or highlights actions that they could have taken months or years before. This is not to imply that such action is easy to do. It is not. However, doing something is preferable to doing nothing. Weick explains why he believes this to be the case. "Action... clarifies what the organization is doing, what business it is in, and what its projects may be. Inaction... is more puzzling and more senseless: there is a greater likelihood for bizarre meanings to be attached and for an unhealthy amount of autism to be introduced. Actions, in other words, provide tangible items that can be attended to... In the absence of action, any act of reflection is directed toward relatively unfilled periods of lived experience. This means that to find a filled period of action that can be made sensible, the reflection must push farther back in time and fixate on more dated experience. Since the experience is even farther out of touch with current happenings, the likelihood of misinterpretation is increased... Thus, when there is confusion and some member of a group asks, 'What should I do?' and some other member says, 'I don't know, just do something,' that's probably a much better piece of advice than you might realize"[4]. Stated simply, action provides managers with first hand experience from which to make sense of complex events. Inaction at best is speculation, fabrication or mental masturbation.

These four pieces of advice governing change practices make it easier to take action and to do something. The model is, thus, a blueprint for capitalizing on an immediate and obvious improvement opportunity that has been avoided or ignored (i.e., the dinosaur in the living room). Since mistakes can evolve into confusing arrays of activities, a management team can use the suggested methods and practices to unravel the ball of yarn and to gain insight (gleaned through action) into improving performance. Even if the team is not clear, management can still start the process and get the ball rolling:

1. Determine the opportunities that exist to improve performance. These opportunities tend to be the ones that persist despite all prior attempts to kill them. Think of it as *"Night of the Living Dead"*. Such issues keep popping up regardless of the topic discussed. These are the issues that most likely warrant immediate attention. These are the big ugly truths you're been ignoring and avoiding. These are the dinosaurs in the living room. If senior executives ignore the changes that everyone knows should be made, they will have little credibility. Moreover, when the management team asks its employees to do more or to try harder, the staff will give no legitimacy to the request. And leaders need legitimacy from followers in order to lead. For example:

Shortly after a diversified manufacturer was acquired, a new CEO was installed. Revenues were shrinking. The company suffered from a dilution of resources spread across incompatible business units. Overseas competition infringed on the existing customer base. And, most important, the company lacked the technical resources needed to compete more effectively in niche applications and markets. During an employee meeting, the CEO presented a sharply focused strategy, and explained the organization would undergo a series of redesign and streamlining efforts. The improvements aimed at fixing its core work processes and eliminating non-value-added work. When the floor opened for questions a senior engineer asked, "You say that you want to become more technical. What plans exist to bolster the technical side of the house? We've been waiting for the day that senior management decided whether it really wants to be a high tech firm". The CEO never directly answered the question and implied that there were no plans in the works to address the single most pressing problem the company faced year after year. The reason was due to the lack of revenue to support additional staff. Everything that was said, thereafter, was ignored. The employees had heard the same response every year. Budgets did not allow for adding staff even though they all knew that the lack of revenue was because customers lacked confidence in the company's technical ability. Within a few months after the meeting, a rash of resignations – all from engineering- ensued. Leaders do not get many chances to establish legitimacy. Do not squander the opportunities – literally or figuratively!

2. *Convene a working session of the senior managers.* The purpose of this session is several-fold. First, the management team decides what changes they will enact. For example, if the company departed from the original success formula for the wrong reasons, the management team must decide to re-establish the focus and/or prior business model and figure out what to do with those pieces/parts that no longer fit. If the company needs to pare the base of unprofitable customers, products or both, then the management team needs to make that decision. For example, when the VP of Marketing assumed the leadership as the President, he knew what had to be done. He convened a meeting of his senior

staff; presented data that showed that too many products were unprofitable; explained that absorbing burden was no longer going to be the primary strategy; and that it was time to face up to the realization that the business was actually smaller than people thought it was. The team made the decision in a single afternoon to exit a product line and to install more rigorous criteria that orders would now have to meet. In addition, they decided that market share would no longer be the major driver of the business. Instead, earnings before interest, taxes and depreciation would serve as the main measure of success. Such decisions are, oftentimes, policy changes, and the leader must ensure that: a) everyone buys into the decision or that minimum agreement exists before anyone leaves the room; and b) the entire organization knows these decisions and what the implications are. Once decisions are made, the team then determines what actions are needed to effect the change, expel the dinosaur or to reverse the decline in performance. Toward these ends, they need to shape an overall framework and implementation strategy; identify the high level opportunities for improvement to tackle; set measurable targets; and assign individuals within the organization accountability for actually effecting the changes. In so far as possible, the scope of the plans should be incremental in nature such that the organization can reasonably absorb the changes without getting overwhelmed.

3. Launch a business improvement process. The next step is to launch an organized and orchestrated business improvement process. The purpose is to translate the targeted opportunities into actions that will generate immediate results – not more discussion. This requires the management team to consider three important levels of the overall business improvement process: content, process and context[5].

The Dinosaur in the Living Room

<u>Content</u>: In so far as possible, the business improvement effort should be tailored to reflect the nature of the performance challenge. For example, if the opportunity is to reduce fixed costs, then the *content* of the improvement effort might be organized around related elements such as fixed assets, overhead, accounts receivable and/or inventory. If the content of the improvement opportunity is to increase revenue, then the effort might organize around products, services and/or sales channels. It may sound obvious, but the *content* of the improvement effort must match the nature of the challenge. This means that the management team should have the end in mind and know what metrics they want to affect. Too often, a management team will overlook the *content* and move straight to problem solving before framing the challenge or breaking the topic into its component parts. Ignoring content will tend to replace causal variables with intermediate ones that have little or no chance to produce results.

<u>Process</u>: The *process* must, likewise, be aligned or matched with the improvement opportunity. Toward this end, it helps to be clear about the design and method by which results will be achieved. For example, one company found that its installed base had grown significantly over the years while new products sales declined. The prior management team had only half heartedly allocated resources to address the higher margin aftermarket business. Once a theoretical potential was calculated to compare current performance and to determine revenue expectations, the new president launched eight short burst, projects teams focused on boosting the sales of five new products; opening two new sales channels; and reducing the backlog of aftermarket orders. He asked the aftermarket sales manager to create a scorecard and matrix that tracked product sales by channel. In addition, customers were

segmented into three tiers and assigned to the appropriate sales channel. A migration chart that graphically showed four stages of account development and market penetration was created. This action set the stage for designing account strategies tailored to the specifics of each customer.

In contrast to this more involved and sophisticated improvement process, one company discovered that its pricing policy caused millions of dollars of margin to erode because it was more concerned with market share and discounting. In this instance, the policy needed to be changed and communicated effectively. In yet another case, the opportunity to reduce total material cost required the involvement of a company and several of its suppliers. Since the players were geographically dispersed and could not practically have frequent interaction, a two-day workshop was created. The session consisted of five inter-company teams from three different organizations, each focused on a different aspect of material cost (e.g., packaging, transportation, leveraging purchasing power, alternate materials and de-contenting & product standardization). Since time was short, each team had to identify 2-3 specific opportunities for improving results by the end of the first day and present these to the leader of each business. The business leaders from each company had to decide on the spot which recommendations had merit and were approved. By the end of the second day, each team developed a short term goal for each approved recommendation; and then drafted a preliminary action plan with due dates and individual assignments. These were presented at the end of the second day to the same leaders of each company and were either approved or revised on the spot.

As can be seen, each business improvement *process* was shaped according to the improvement opportunity and to the nature of the challenge. The process can be involved and sophisticated; or it can require a simple or single action like a policy change that acts as a catalyst that triggers other changes. It can warrant individual action; or involve cross functional teams; or it can even cross over organizational boundaries and involve customers and suppliers, if needed.

Context: Unlike content or process, context is more difficult to assess and therefore harder to align with the business improvement process. *Context*, used here, refers to the ability and willingness of the organization to tackle the business improvement process. Understanding the *context* enables a management team to set the pace of change and to determine the scope/size of the effort. This means that senior management must be attentive to the conditions that will enhance or inhibit the ability and willingness to launch a change process. For example, a tier one automotive supplier was in danger of losing repeat business due to late deliveries, cost overruns and technical problems. A quick assessment revealed what everyone already knew; that the product development process was not being followed and that the quality gates were being circumvented. Closer review showed that of forty-three work processes that comprised the overall product development process, fourteen were incomplete; eighteen needed revision or updating; and eight of the steps that comprised some of the core secondary processes had no one assigned primary accountability to perform the task. At the time the assessment was done, the staff was embroiled in two product launches and three new quotes. It is safe to say that the capacity of this company was severely limited. Under circumstances such as these, senior management would be better served to target a few core work processes to repair. In fact, that's exactly what they did. A small team of engineering, quality, manufacturing and program management professionals targeted ten core work processes (e.g., prototype builds, design to target pricing, single, simultaneous product & process release, etc.) to redesign and fix, one process at a time. They established themselves as an audit team, started to evaluate existing programs against the standards they set, and worked with others side-by-side to implement the required changes, thereby, ensuring that the product development process was followed.

As this case shows, the ability and willingness of the company to tackle a large scale change process was unlikely to happen given its history and current workload. To accommodate the situation, the team used a punctuated strategy by sequencing the change process. They narrowed the scope to only ten of forty-three core work processes they knew were most critical. They modified the pace so that only one work process was worked on at a time. By adjusting the scope and pace of the business improvement process, they began to improve performance incrementally.

4. Ensure that each team fully completes the assignment. This means that the team must exit any negative spirals that exist and undo any adverse decisions and replace them with positive changes. The purpose, here, is to break the tie between competing elements and fully extricate the organization from a course of action that splits its focus. The job is not complete until the improvements are sustainable. Once it is clear that the first wave of improvements is locked in, the next step is to expand the scope and financial impact of the effort. Building capability by terracing improvement activity can strengthen an organization's capacity to absorb greater change. For example, one company started by launching three short burst teams. Each team focused on departmental improvements. Once they showed the results were real and sustainable, senior

The Dinosaur in the Living Room

management asked that they broaden the scope and financial impact. At the same time these three teams kept working, management launched a cross functional effort aimed at eliminating non-value-added work. Although these efforts were unrelated to the initial projects, it, nonetheless, freed up time to work on the top priorities. For the next two years management focused on reversing the negative spiral connected to the dinosaur… while systematically unburdening the staff by streamlining work processes.

One note of caution is, when you finally decide to tackle the obvious and to expel the dinosaur from your midst; please do not look outside the organization for magic bullets. First, they do not exist. Second, you need to clean up your own messes. Third, unless you are directly involved, you will not derive the learning that is so important for future applications. There is nothing more frustrating than people who do not stick around long enough for their mistakes to catch up to them. As a result, they never learn the lessons that are crucial to effective management. Delegating tough changes of this nature to outsiders simply is another form of avoidance. Therefore, insiders must do the implementation.

Final Comments

As my children were growing up, like most kids, they periodically lamented the fact that they were not as good of athletes as they had hoped to be in certain sports; or that they were not as good of a student in school that semester as they had wanted to be; or that someone else was better at something to which they aspired and wanted to excel. When confronted with the obvious disappointment I saw in their faces and heard in their voices, I tried to console them with a story about a famous teacher and scholar. The teacher lay in tears on his deathbed. His students who surrounded him inquired, "Why are you crying? Is it because you did not become as great of a person as some other scholars did?" "No", he said. "Is it because you were not able to accomplish more in your lifetime?" Again he said, "No". Then is that you left something unfinished?" the students asked. "No", he lamented. "Then why do you cry?" his students implored. The scholar answered, "It is because I did not become more of who I already was". Organizations have similar regrets. They have the potential to become more of what they already are. They possess the ability, know-how and even readiness, but act in contradiction to their best instincts and information that is readily available. The irony is that the opportunity to achieve a higher level of performance is within their grasp, if management would just step through the door and act. Waiting until an organization is on its deathbed… is one way to infuse urgency or to signal that it's time to get the lead out. Then again, it might be too late to make a difference. Yes, it takes courage to acknowledge mistakes. Given some of the scandals that occurred in business, it is probably an understatement. Most people gravitate to positive and reaffirming events and shy away from negative and disconfirming ones. To some, acting accountable is second nature. To others, attributing accountability to factors outside their control is primary to their nature. However, confronting a dinosaur in the living room is a group level construct, and not just an individual dynamic. It is a case where the management team collectively knows what to do, but colludes in their inaction. It is a case where the change involved does not require a radical alteration of the entire organization. It is a case where taking focused action in punctuated, short bursts will produce both results and learning. It is a case where doing nothing has higher risks than doing something. It is a case where acting

The Dinosaur in the Living Room

on the obvious will have clear and positive consequences. Such arguments create a compelling case for action…

I recall an interview that one of the television networks conducted with an NFL football coach that seemed to capture the essence of the foregoing discussion. The coach had just assumed control of offensive play calling from his assistant coach. Before he assumed responsibility for the offense, the team averaged a paltry 13 points per game. After he started calling the offensive plays, the team averaged 27 points per game and got into the playoffs as a result. During the interview he was asked how he achieved double the output. He explained, "You know this game is really quite simple and the job of coaching is easier than it looks. Please do not tell anyone that. I simplified the plays, eliminated the complexity and I let the talent on the field make it happen". Managers can take a page from the coach's playbook by first facing up to and confronting the dinosaur in the living room, and secondly, by implementing the obvious actions needed to change it. It truly is that straightforward!

Endnotes:

Chapter One

1. Cohen, H. 1998. The Performance Paradox, Academy of Management Executive, Volume 12, No. 3
2. Bakker, R. 1986. The Dinosaur Heresies. William Morrow & Company. New York, New York
3. Cleveland Enterprise Magazine; 1997. The 90's M&A Craze: Everybody's in on the Act, Summer 1997, 22.
4. Schaffer, R. 1991. Results Improvement is the Key to Creativity and Empowerment. Journal of Quality and Participation, September.
5. Harvey, J., 1974. The Abilene Paradox : The Management of Agreement, Organizational Dynamics. Summer.
6. Shaw, M & Blum, J. 1965. Group performance as a function of task difficulty and the group's awareness of member satisfaction. Journal of Applied psychology 49:151-154
7. Argyris, C. 1994. Good Communication that Blocks Learning. Harvard Business Review, July-August.
8. Weick, K. 1979. The Social Psychology of Organizing. Addison Wesley Publishing Company. Menlo Park, California
9. Ibid
10. Ibid
11. Ffeiffer, J. and Sutton, R. 2000. The Knowing Doing Gap; Harvard Business School Press; Boston, MA
12. Ibid
13. Kotter, J. 1996. Leading Change, Harvard Business School Press, Boston, MA

Chapter Two

1. Micklethwait, J. and Wooldrdge, A. 1996; The Witch Doctors; Times Books, New York, New York
2. Christian, C. & Raynor, M. 2003, The Innovators Solution, Harvard Business School Press, Boston, MA
3. Hamel, G. and Prahalad, C.K.; 1994; Competing for the Future; The Harvard Business School Press, Boston, MA.
4. "The Fortune 500", Fortune Magazine, April 18, 1994
5. Micklethwait, J. and Wooldridge, A. 1996; The Witch Doctors; Times Books, New York, New York
6. Ashkenas, R. and Francis, S. Integration Managers: Special Leaders for Special Times; Harvard Business Review; November-December, 2000
7. Christiansen, C. The Innovators Dilemma; 1997; Harvard Business School Press; Boston, MA
8. Heskett, J., Sasser, E., and Schlessinger, L.; The Service Profit Chain; The Free Press, New York, New York; 1997
9. Ibid
10. Boardroom Reports; 1992; All About Continuous Improvement, July 21: 9
11. Ibid
12. Nohria, N and Berkley, J.; Whatever Happened to the Take Charge Manager; Harvard Business Review; January-February; 1994
13. Beer, M. Eisenstat, R. and Spector, B. 1990. The Critical Path to Corporate Renewal, Harvard Business School Press, Cambridge, MA
14. Nohria, N and Berkley, J.; Whatever Happened to the Take Charge Manager; Harvard Business Review; January-February; 1994

15. Schein, E. The Anxiety of Learning, Harvard Business Review, March 2002
16. An installed base strategy is an option when the ratios of the products that already exist in the field far outnumber new product sales. As such, the profit on initial product sales is slim. However, the margins of follow-on products and services are much more attractive. The objective is to build as large an installed base as possible to invite follow-on revenue and higher profits.

Chapter Three

1. Moore, J. Living on the Fault Line. Harper Business. New York, New York. 2000
2. Slywotzky, A. Value Migration. Harvard Business School Press. Boston, MA 1996
3. Porter, M. What is Strategy, Harvard Business Review. November-December 1996.
4. Whitney, J. Strategic Renewal for Business Units. Harvard Business Review. July-August 1996.
5. Robert, M. Strategy Pure and Simple. McGraw Hill Inc. New York, New York. 1993.
6. Tregoe, B. & Zimmerman, J. Top Management Strategy. Simon & Schuster Inc. New York, New York. 1980.
7. Hamel, G. & Prahalid, C.K. Competing for the Future. Harvard Business School Press. Boston, MA. 1994
8. Whitney, J. Strategic Renewal for Business Units. Harvard Business Review. July-August 1996.
9. Ibid

10. Collins, J. & Porras, J. Built to Last, HarperBusiness, New York, NY 1994
11. Buckingham, M. & Coffman, C, First Break All the Rules, Simon & Schuster New York, New York, 1999
12. Kegan, R. & Lahey, L. The Real Reason Why People Won't Change, Harvard Business Review, November 2001
13. Ibid
14. Ibid
15. Porter, M. What is Strategy, Harvard Business Review. November-December 1996.
16. Card, O.S. The Memory of Earth, Tor Books, New York, NY 1992

Chapter Four

1. Bakker, R. 1986. The Dinosaur Heresies. William Morrow & Company. New York, New York
2. Schaffer, R. The Breakthrough Strategy, Harper Business, New York, NY 1988
3. Kotter, J. Leading Change, Harvard Business School Press, Boston MA. 1996
4. Collins, J. & Porras, J. Built to Last, Harper Business, New York, NY 1994
5. Ibid
6. Slater, R. Get Better or Get Beaten, Irwin Professional Publishing, New York, New York, 1994
7. Kim, W.C. & Mauborgne, R. Value Innovation: The Strategic Logic of High Growth, Harvard Business Review January-February 1997

[8] Burns, D. Feeling Good – The New Mood Therapy, Penguin Books Inc., New York, New York, 1981
[9] Mitroff, I. Stakeholders of the Organizational Mind, Jossey-Bass, San Francisco, California 1983
[10] Mitroff, I. and Mason, R. "Structuring Ill-Structured Policy Issues: Further Explorations in a Methodology for Messy Problems." Strategic Management Journal, 1980
[11] Schein, E. The Anxiety of Learning, Harvard Business Review, March 2002
[12] Burns, D. Feeling Good – The New Mood Therapy, Penguin Books Inc., New York, New York, 1981
[13] Ibid
[14] Ibid
[15] Burns, D. Feeling Good – The New Mood Therapy, Penguin Books Inc., New York, New York, 1981
[16] Ibid
[17] Ibid
[18] Ibid
[19] Weick, K. The Social Psychology of Organizing, Addison Wesley Publishing, Reading, Massachusetts, 1979
[20] Kegan, R. & Lahey, L. The Real Reason Why People Won't Change, Harvard Business Review, November 2001
[21] Ibid
[22] Ibid
[23] Porter, M. What is Strategy, Harvard Business Review. November-December 1996.

Chapter Five

[1] Eldridge, Niles & Gould, J. "Punctuated Equilibria: an alternative to phyletic gradualism," in Schopf, TJM., ed., Models in Paleobiology, San Francisco: Freeman Cooper 1972

[2] Bakker, R. 1986. The Dinosaur Heresies. William Morrow & Company. New York, New York
[3] Cohen, H. 1998. The Performance Paradox, Academy of Management Executive, Volume 12, No. 3
[4] Ashkenas, R. The Organization's New Clothes. In Hesselbein, F. Goldsmith, M. & Beckhard, R., (eds.), The Organization for the Future: San Francisco: Jossey Bass. 1995
[5] Baghai,M., Coley, S. & White, D. The Alchemy of Growth, Perseus Publishing, New York, New York 1999
[6] Ibid
[7] Beer, M. Eisenstat, R. and Spector, B. 1990. The Critical Path to Corporate Renewal, Harvard Business School Press, Cambridge, MA
[8] Cohen, H. 1998. The Performance Paradox, Academy of Management Executive, Volume 12, No. 3
[9] Weick, K. Small Wins in Organizational Life. Dividend. Winter: 2-6, 1993
[10] Collins, J. & Porras, J. Built to Last, Harper Collins Publishing Inc. 1994
[11] Ibid
[12] Schaffer, R. High Impact Consulting, Jossey Bass Publishing, San Francisco, California, 1997
[13] Sull, D. Why Good Companies Go Bad, Harvard Business Review, July/August, 1999
[14] Collins, J. Turning Goals into Results: The Power of Catalytic Mechanisms, Harvard Business Review, July/August, 1999
[15] Gilbert, C & Bower, J. Disruptive Change, When Trying Harder is Part of the Problem, Harvard Business Review, May 2002
[16] Ibid

17. Schaffer, R. The Breakthrough Strategy, Harper Business, New York, NY 1988
18. Covey, Steven. The Seven Habits of Highly Successful People, Fireside Edition, Simon & Schuster Publishing, New York, New York, 1990
19. Sarafino, E. Principles of Behavior Change, John Wiley & Sons, Inc. New York, New York, 1996

Chapter Six

1. Bakker, R. The Dinosaur Heresies, William Morrow & Company, New York, NY, 1986
2. Ibid
3. Ackoff, R. Redesigning the Future, John Wiley & Sons Publishing, New York, NY 1974
4. Weick, K. The Social Psychology of Organizing, Addison Wesley Publishing, Reading, Massachusetts, 1979.
5. Ibid
6. Pfeffer, J. & Sutton, R. The Knowing Doing Gap, Harvard Business School Press, Boston Massachusetts, 2000
7. Schaffer, R. The Breakthrough Strategy, Harper Business, New York, N.Y. 1988
8. Rogers, P. Holland, T. & Haas, D. Value Acceleration: Lessons for the Masters, Harvard Business Review, 2002
9. Ibid
10. Rogers, P. Holland, T. & Haas, D. Lessons from Private Equity Masters, Harvard Business Review, June 2002
11. Ibid
12. Argyris, C. Why Individuals and Organizations Have Difficulty in Double Loop Learning

[13] Ibid
[14] Martin, R. Changing the Mind of the Corporation, Harvard Business Review, November/December 1993
[15] Ibid
[16] Argyris, C. & Schon, D. Organizational Learning, Addison Wesley Publishers, Reading, Mass. 1978
[17] Ibid
[18] Collins, J. & Porras, J. Built to Last, Harper Business Division, Harper Collins Publishers 1994

Chapter Seven

[1] Coutu, D. How Resilience Works, Harvard Business Review, May 2002
[2] Christiansen, C. & Raynor, M. Why Hard Nosed Executives Should Care About Management Theory, Harvard Business Review, September 2003
[3] Pfeffer, J. & Sutton, R. The Knowing Doing Gap, Harvard Business School Press, Boston Massachusetts, 2000
[4] Weick, K. The Social Psychology of Organizing, Addison Wesley Publishing Company, 1979
[5] Neilsen, E. Becoming an OD Practitioner; Prentice Hall, Inc, Englewood Cliffs, New Jersey; 1984

About The Author

Harlow Cohen has thirty-two years of consulting, management and academic experience. He is the president of HBC&A, Inc., a change management consulting firm, and an adjunct professor at Case Western Reserve University. His consulting spans clients in automotive, industrial, consumer products, retail, research, insurance and banking. Before forming HBC&A, he was a senior consultant for Robert H. Schaffer and Associates, VP of Organization Planning and Development for Ameritrust Company, Senior VP of Operations for Boykin Management and Director of Human Resources for Cole National Corporation and Cole Consumer Products.

Dr. Cohen holds a Ph.D. in Organizational Behavior and a Masters in Organization Development from Case Western Reserve University. He has published articles on achieving positive results, identifying and developing managerial high performers, fostering effective teams and boosting the contributions of human resource professionals.

Made in the USA